Endorsements for *A Tail of Hope's* ....

This is a compassionate tale of healing and is a treat to read for any pet owner searching for healing methods that reach beyond the physical.

—Dana Scott, editor in chief, *Dogs Naturally* magazine

It was a pleasure to read this heart-centered offering about Hope, a dear companion, and other animals in Diane Weinmann's healing practice. Diane demonstrated a lovely way to support our animals who are experiencing health issues, disease, trauma, and aging. Her knowledge and studies of holistic practices and her cooperative integration of traditional veterinary care are commendable. This is a must-read for those seeking additional ways of helping their animals and to develop an effective animal-human bond.

—Carol Komitor, founder, Healing Touch for Animals

Ms. Weinmann has written a very touching story of Hope, a family dog that became an inspiration for her family as she traversed a series of illnesses. With Ms. Weinmann's assistance she returned in the form of another puppy they named Faith. You will be moved by what truly is a story of hope and faith, as well as the dogs themselves, Hope and Faith.

—Dr. Steven Farmer, author *Animal Spirit Guides* and *Earth Magic*

An inspiring and heartfelt story about a deeply beloved dog named Hope and how an animal communicator uses her love, skill, and divine assistance to help Hope's family through the process of finding her as she returns to earth to be reunited. Of the many touching moments, my favorite is when Hope—now renamed Faith—immediately kisses her human mom on the nose when they meet, which is precisely what she asked for as a sign. Enjoy this poignant, true story of a dog's life, death, and rebirth—surrounded by the devotion and love of her family and a dedicated animal communicator at each stage.

—Teresa Wagner, animal communicator and grief counselor

Diane is truly a gifted storyteller, communicator, and healer. Once you read her story about Hope, all you have ever questioned will be answered. This book is a life-changing journey we all need to take.

—Kristin Payden, RVT, HTAP
Specialized care manager for JoyCares
Personalized Pet Care LLC.

Diane Weinmann has a gift. I have seen this for many years now, and she continues to amaze me. The most admirable quality is that she shares this gift over and over. Now her gifts reside in the pages of a book. If you have ever had an animal, this book will touch your heart, enlighten, and educate. Diane put into words what we all have gone through being the guardians of our beloved pets. Enjoy and savor this beautiful story and hope she comes out with another very soon!

—Kim Wasielewski, ATP Reiki master
Angel Inspirations
www.Angel-inspirations.com

One thing that I have learned over my career of fourteen years caring for animals is that mixing a holistic/alternative therapy approach in conjunction with veterinarian care is not only important for the animal but just as important for the pet parent. Diane has really opened up my eyes, and I have seen firsthand that adding the holistic modalities along with the veterinarian care makes a huge difference in the medical journey of any animal. Diane has a gift, and her journey with Hope is a true testimonial. I am blessed to have her on our team as the alternative therapy provider for JoyCares Personalized Pet Care. She works closely with our specialized care manager, Kris Payden, and I am comforted to know that she provides our clients with peace of mind when they are dealing with some heartbreaking and stressful situations with their cherished pet. Everyone always tells me that they wonder what their animal is thinking; they wish that their animal could talk and tell them what they need. Diane provides that for our pet parents and then swings into action to give their pet everything that they have asked for.

—Joy Sutton, founder, JoyCares Personalized Pet
Care, LLC http://www.joycares.com/

A Tail of Hope's Faith

DIANE WEINMANN

BALBOA.
PRESS
A DIVISION OF HAY HOUSE

Author Credits:
Diane Weinmann is an award winning writer who has written articles for Animal Wellness and Dog's Naturally Magazines. She publishes a monthly newsletter from her business, For the Love of Animals. Subscribe to her newsletter at www.theloveofanimals.com.

Balboa Press books may be ordered through booksellers or by contacting:

Balboa Press
A Division of Hay House
1663 Liberty Drive
Bloomington, IN 47403
www.balboapress.com
1 (877) 407-4847

Because of the dynamic nature of the Internet, any web addresses or links contained in this book may have changed since publication and may no longer be valid. The views expressed in this work are solely those of the author and do not necessarily reflect the views of the publisher, and the publisher hereby disclaims any responsibility for them.

The author of this book does not dispense medical advice or prescribe the use of any technique as a form of treatment for physical, emotional, or medical problems without the advice of a physician, either directly or indirectly. The intent of the author is only to offer information of a general nature to help you in your quest for emotional and spiritual well-being. In the event you use any of the information in this book for yourself, which is your constitutional right, the author and the publisher assume no responsibility for your actions.

Printed in the United States of America.

ISBN: 978-1-4525-9992-2 (sc)
ISBN: 978-1-4525-9993-9 (hc)
ISBN: 978-1-4525-9999-1 (e)

Library of Congress Control Number: 2014921724

Balboa Press rev. date: 12/11/2014

To all the animals I have had the pleasure of speaking with, helped, or healed, along with Milo, Tink-R-Belle, Kelsey, Hope, and Faith. I look forward to my future where I continue to learn and grow from all my forthcoming animal teachers. It is my honor and privilege to have known these animal friends and to serve them. I promise to do my very best to assist them in some way in order to improve their emotional or physical health and present circumstances.

Contents

Preface

As an animal communicator and healer, I have had many miraculous experiences. I firmly believe that pet owners would benefit from hearing and learning about how to deal with the joy, love, and ultimate loss of a beloved animal friend.

The knowledge that I have gained from talking to our animal companions astounds me. More importantly, through my thirteen years as an animal communicator and my ten-plus years as an energy healer, I know that I have important information to provide to those that have an animal friend. This information should be especially welcome if they have had the heart-wrenching loss of a beloved pet or are currently going through one of the worst times in their life—trying to help a pet that has been diagnosed as terminal.

My spirit guides always told me that I had a book inside me, but I was not to write it just yet. As frustrated as I felt, I kept asking when I would write it, not knowing what I would write about. At the beginning of 2013, out of the clear blue, I was told through my psychic mentor that I was to write my book. The problem was that I still didn't know what I should write about. I'd had so many experiences and so much to say that I wasn't sure what to focus on. Not to worry—spirit provided again. I received a clear message that the name of the book was to be *A Tail of Hope's Faith*. Yep, they even showed me how *tail* was to be written. In the title was my answer. I was to write Hope's story. I had just come full circle in an amazing true story of one dog's battle against the inevitable and her triumph through reincarnation to return to those she loved.

Let me say from the start that I believe very deeply in animal hospice. I believe our animals should be consulted on their life wishes. They should have a voice in how and when they will transition into spirit. Based on this belief, I have talked to and assisted many of my pet clients and their owners through the hardest decisions of their lives.

Before speaking with our animal friends, I call upon my spirit guides, Saint Francis of Assisi, and my animal totems to ensure that my communication is clear, accurate, and for the highest good of everyone involved. I let the owners and their animal friends guide me to receive messages of hope, healing, and pure love, working to ensure that everyone involved understands what is being conveyed and how to help.

Acknowledgments

I have been blessed by many family, friends, and animals in my life. I wish to thank my husband, Herb, my son, Corey, twin sister, Debbie, our parents, who have passed into spirit and my niece Janelle for their constant love and support. They put up with me and continue to love me no matter how crazy I sound at times. What I do is hard to fathom for some, and their belief in me speaks volumes.

I wish to thank my healing group, Theresa, Bonnie, Donna, Tammy, and my best friends, Susan and Wendy, for everything they taught me in life. It's been a wild ride, one which I anticipate will only get better. I look forward to the future, because it is so comforting to know that you are unconditionally supported.

My gratitude goes out to all my past and future animal teachers for allowing me into their minds, bodies, and hearts. Without them, I would not be able to do what I do. They have all been the light in my life, my reason for being, and I will continue to honor our connection for the rest of my lifetime. My only hope is that I serve them as well as they have served me.

Lastly, I send my endless love and gratitude to Rosanne and her family for allowing me into their lives. The opportunity to know their dog Hope in her life, death, and reincarnation back to the family has truly been an amazing gift, and I will cherish it in my heart forever. I want to give a million thanks to Rosanne for all her help in bringing this book into fruition. I know how very hard it was to relive the ending moments of Hope's life, but her story needed to be told. She deserved it. I am so very glad we told it together.

Introduction

What would you do for your beloved animal companions if they were sick? How far would you go to help them? What if you knew a way to hear their thoughts, how they really felt inside even though they couldn't talk out loud? Would you want to know what they think? Would you want to know what they were physically feeling? If they were in pain would you want to know?

This book is a true story of dedication, love, and perseverance on the part of a dog named Hope, her family, and an animal communicator. Through animal communication, specific holistic healing, and the diligent assistance of her family, we were able to extend Hope's last days and ensure a good quality of life. Hope was able to express her thoughts and feelings, and we consequently provided healing and guidance in a very difficult situation. Together, we made Hope's life better. This I know, because she told me.

In reading this story, you will learn how animal communication can help any situation between you and your pet. You will come to know what healing modalities can assist your animal, whether your pet simply pulled a muscle, has arthritis, or had something more life threatening. I will explain how the use of aromatherapy using essential oils can reduce symptoms and create changes in your pet's behavior. I will teach you how to utilize tuning forks to provide sound and vibration therapy for your pet to elicit relaxation, speed wound healing, help with their range of motion, ground your pet, and help to provide focus for them.

I will explain the difference between Reiki energy healing and Healing Touch for Animals (HTA) and provide much-needed information regarding the energy system of your animal companion. I cannot provide step-by-step instructions for HTA techniques, because that is proprietary information; however, if you are interested, there will be URLs listed in the additional resource section of this book to guide you to a class in your area where you can obtain instruction. Such classes were by far the best learning experience I have ever had in my entire life, and it helped shape who I am and what I do today.

Additionally, I will show you how to use Bach Flower essences to help with end-of-life emotional issues for both you and your pet, along with using them to provide comfort to an animal when they have a debilitating illness. I will also provide instruction for healing with color.

Hope had a rough beginning to her life, but she didn't have a rough end. The love she received from her human family and their dedication to helping her was a true testament to their belief that she deserved a chance just as much as a human being. She was a valuable family member who warranted all the care, love, support, and healing they would provide.

I am humbled and proud to have been part of her journey, and my life is richer for having known her. Thank you, Hope; you have provided me, your family, and everyone who knows your story with the essence of your name—Hope.

Hope and the Family

In November 2004, in a one-dog family that also included a rabbit and two cats, Rosanne Sopko, the mother of three children, decided to go back to work full-time. The children living with her and her husband in their Cleveland suburb were Mitch, a boy of fifteen, and her youngest son, Mackenzie, who was four weeks shy of turning fourteen. In addition to the boys, Rosanne's daughter, Jessica, was sixteen. Rosanne had not worked full-time for many years. This was a big decision that she did not make easily. That in itself was scary, but to top it off, she would be leaving her pets alone all day. This was indeed a big change for them. Their dog, Murray, had been adopted two years prior and had always had someone home with him. Now he would be left alone most of the day, and that did not sit right with the family. As a result, the search for a companion began.

Mitch, Rosanne's eldest son, went online to search for a pet to save. He used the same website for the local Cleveland Animal Protective League on Willey Avenue that he'd used when he'd found Murray. Murray had been given up at the age of nine months by his previous owners because of physical deformities that needed surgery. That didn't bother the Sopkos. Murray, with his long, black curly fur, was a great addition to their home, and they felt that another rescue dog would work out equally well.

The Sopkos found two puppies online and couldn't decide between a male and a female dog. The boy puppy looked like Nipper, the RCA dog. For those of you not old enough to remember the RCA dog, his body was mostly white with dark ears, and his head was always tilted as if he were listening. Very cute! He was part Jack Russell and part fox terrier and received his name because he would bite at the backs of people's legs—not a legacy the family wanted to repeat. This dog had been left to fend for himself—without food or water—in a foreclosed house.

The girl puppy was three months old, and she had a very compelling story. She'd been abandoned by her owners and left out in the cold November weather. The animal warden had picked her up off a freeway (where she was almost run over by a car) and had taken her to a kennel. Because of this incident, the dog was extremely fearful of people. She was not a good candidate for adoption. She tried to hide in the corner of her kennel and didn't interact with anyone. She was very unhappy and scared. She didn't understand where she was or what was happening. Being in a strange place (on top of her recent abandonment) was almost too much for her to bear. She was negatively acting out, which would not be in her best interest, but she didn't realize what was about to occur.

The workers at the shelter determined that the female puppy should be euthanized, because she was afraid and belly growled when anyone came near her. In a no-kill shelter, this would never be an option, but in a shelter where dogs and cats are valued only for their looks and personalities, this puppy was doomed. No-kill shelters try to rehabilitate or train a dog using positive rewards, but other types of shelters may not have the time or the funds to employ these methods.

In spite of the female puppy's problems, a miracle happened. A warmhearted individual spotted the scared orphaned puppy that was scheduled to be put down and fought to save her. She saw potential and was determined that this dog would not be put to death! This kind lady saved the puppy's life.

The lady decided that she would take the dog and place her in a foster home with five cats. This may seem like an unusual choice, but it worked for this dog. The new pup seemed to fit right in with the cats and became comfortable in her temporary home. The cats liked their new playmate and treated her as if she were just another cat. As you can imagine, at her young age, the puppy was very impressionable. Having cats for playmates was not exactly ideal, but she was home—for now. Her foster family stated that she was adjusting well and was showing no signs of aggression, but she was painfully shy. The puppy loved all her new toys and treats and had never been treated to such kindness before. She even had her own little bed. She must have thought she was in heaven.

The foster family was a single mom with two little children, and the mom was active with a cat rescue. The foster mom named the puppy Hope, because she was hopeful that Hope would find a forever home. The shelter website stated that she was available for adoption to a special person or family. In order to increase interest in the puppy, the local shelter published a description of her in their weekly column in the local newspaper. *"Ruff, ruff.* My name is Hope, and I need a home and someone to love me. I am a German shepherd/retriever mix, a medium-size dog, mostly brown. I am a female puppy, already spayed; good with kids, dogs, and cats." Then the article described the way the shelter came to obtain Hope. There was one strange thing about Hope's listing, though. She was listed in the *feline* section. Coincidence? Not on your life! The little puppy was slowly being turned into a cat.

After accidentally finding a dog under the cat section of the website, Rosanne and her family were intrigued with Hope's story and wanted to meet her. This meeting took more than a week to arrange, but they did it. Rosanne was very nervous. She felt the adoption process was difficult and time consuming. Rosanne learned that two other families were interested in Hope, and the adoption counselor had to interview all three families before making a decision based on the best choice for Hope's forever home.

Rosanne's family was the last to be interviewed. She took both her sons with her. Most shelters not only require that all of the family members be present but also require that visitation with any other family pets take place prior to approval. Hope was very adorable playing with all the cats and their toys. She was having a great time, but she essentially ignored her visitors. Rosanne and her boys were not deterred. They tried to interact with Hope and kept touching her all over to gauge her reaction. They petted her head, tail, and toes in an attempt to see if she would be receptive or reactive to their touch. Eventually, they all got on the floor with Hope, and she came up to them willingly, sniffing and sniffing. She plopped herself in Mitch's lap to cuddle for a few minutes, and then off she went, chasing a cat.

Rosanne and her boys explained to the adoption counselor that they rescued animals all the time, and when anything with four legs walked through the front door, it stayed! The family explained how they had already adopted one dog who needed special help and would be happy to add to their family of pets. They were all able to hold and hug Hope before they left. The young mom who was fostering the dog for the animal shelter stated that she would review all the interviews and get back to them.

That was the longest week for Rosanne. She almost gave up. She paced. She ranted and raved about why the shelter was not calling. She wanted Hope so badly. She knew that her family would be a great choice. She anticipated having another dog for Christmas, but it looked like it wasn't to be.

Two weeks before Christmas, Rosanne received the long-anticipated phone call. It was the shelter. Rosanne's heart just sank; she was afraid they were calling with bad news, but she quickly became overjoyed to hear that her family was chosen as Hope's forever home. Because her family were the only ones to try to interact with Hope and were so caring and genuine, they were awarded Hope.

Rosanne asked, "When can I have her?" She was very anxious to have that puppy in her arms.

The adoption counselor said, "Whenever you want."

Rosanne promptly replied, "I'll be there within the hour."

Boy, they had a lot to do. Hope needed bowls, leashes, toys, and collars.

Mitch said, "I guess we're going to the pet-supply store with the dog, right?"

"Sure are!" Rosanne ran through the house, picking chewable items up off the floor and putting them out of reach of a young pup. This was going to be a wonderful Christmas.

Rosanne and her two boys drove as fast as they could to pick up Hope. They were so excited to have her. In their arms she went, and they didn't want to put her down. Once they arrived at the pet store, they set her in a shopping cart, and both boys worked from either side of the cart to ensure that the puppy stayed safe while Rosanne pushed. They quickly bought everything needed for the bouncing new addition to their family, all the while showing Hope their treasures for her approval. Tail wagging, she wanted it all!

Once they got home, the family placed Hope on the ground in front of their other dog, Murray, so that the two could meet for the first time. Murray never had trouble getting along with everyone, no matter the species, but Hope had other ideas. Maybe she knew that this was her new home, so she wanted to establish the ground rules right away, but her reaction to Murray was not anticipated. She growled at him, which was comical, because at only three and a half months old, she was a midget compared to Murray. But here she was, telling him what to do. She came in and took over. It was funny to the family, because they never thought a little pip-squeak of a dog would be able to make such a large dog cower, but cower Murray did.

Rosanne's husband commented that he thought she was getting Murray a playmate, but Hope was not a playmate—she was a wife! They all laughed heartily at that.

It wasn't long before Hope's first run to the Animal Emergency Clinic. Only one week after her adoption, this adorable pup swelled from head to toe, so much that her eyes could not open. With Mitch holding Hope tightly, Rosanne drove frantically to the emergency clinic. It seemed that she'd had an allergic reaction to something. But what? After review of all that was fed to Hope or used as a household cleaner that day, Mitch remembered seeing Hope eat a peanut shell that a squirrel had left behind outside. Oh, what a fright and how quickly it all happened. From that day on, the family declared that a bottle of Benadryl was a must-have, and by no means were peanuts or peanut butter allowed to any four-legged animals in or around their home.

Hope settled in nicely with the family, almost as if she'd always been there. Everyone loved her, and she loved them. Murray and Hope became inseparable. They slept together, went outside together, played together. Anytime they were sleeping, Hope would have her head on Murray. Now don't think that

Hope was going soft—oh no! She still ruled the roost. She just decided that whoever she pushed around was still going to be her friend.

Each morning, Murray grabbed a toy in his mouth and greeted the family with his tail wagging. Now, Hope would come along and take the toy from him. Anyone who witnessed her antics was amused, and Murray good-naturedly took it all in stride.

Jackie the bunny was another subject. Because Hope chased the little squirrels in the backyard, the family knew that it was not a good idea to leave her alone with Jackie or to place Jackie on the ground when Hope was around. Jackie would sit on Rosanne's lap, and Hope would lay her nose on Rosanne's leg as if to claim Mom for her own. Hope never harmed Jackie in any way, but she was never given the opportunity to prove to the family that she wouldn't. Rosanne and her family were good pet parents, carefully looking after each pet's well-being.

As Hope matured, she had her own toys, and Murray had his, but for a while, it was a free-for-all. Hope's favorite toy seemed to be a little stuffed blue dog and of course her special bone. She cherished both objects. Her body was very athletic, and she was always running and roughhousing with the boys. She would do a mile run with Rosanne's sons. When Rosanne tried to walk her, it was another story. Attempting to walk the two dogs together was a nightmare. Hope had to be a whole head's length ahead of Murray at all times. Again, the competitive element in her nature reared its ugliness. If Murray ever got in front of Hope, she would menacingly growl at him. Thank goodness Murray liked to pee on everything he saw, so he naturally lagged behind all the time. Needless to say, taking the dogs for a walk was a chore for Rosanne, who was small in stature, but she did enjoy it. Obviously a sucker for punishment!

Hope would always tell Murray when he was out of place. Dirty looks and growling were her means of communication with him. Feeding the dogs together was exciting, as well. Rosanne always had to put Hope's food in her bowl first, and then Murray's. Once both bowls were filled, Rosanne would say, "Enjoy!" and the dogs would dive in with gusto. It was so cute to watch them both wait until given the cue to eat.

Sleeping arrangements were not ideal for Rosanne's husband, Michael. Hope slept between Rosanne and her husband with Murray on the other side of Hope, but both dogs would have their paws pushing her husband off the bed. When Hope was two years old and Murray at eighty pounds, Rosanne's husband put his foot down, and the dogs received their own beds. Wise man—don't know why he waited so long! Murray's place to sleep was designated at the foot of their bed, for he needed the space to sack out full length. As for Hope, she had her bed in the corner of the room. She slept mostly curled up in a circle with her eyes toward the bedroom door in order to watch if anyone entered during the night.

Visitors were another challenge for Hope. Because of her puppyhood experiences, she was not fond of strangers. If she'd known you when she was a puppy, you were okay to enter the house; however, if she didn't, look out! Hope would charge forward, barking excitedly. The family never knew what to expect. If the visitor bent forward toward Hope to make nice with her, she would lunge at him or her. Rosanne had to be extra vigilant when anyone new came around. Even though visitors felt that Hope was harmless, Rosanne was never sure. Prior to the arrival of expected guests or when anyone came to the door, both Murray and Hope would be escorted to Mom and Dad's room, where they would promptly jump on the bed and watch TV. They always had plenty of toys and extra treats in the room to entertain themselves. Hope always listened well and did what she was told.

Toys were great fun for Hope. She loved her squeaky toys. She would use her nose to press down on the toy, squeaking it over and over just to hear the noise it made. She was also a great helper. When Rosanne wanted to vacuum or clean up the house, she would tell Hope to go get her "babies." Hope regarded every toy as a baby unless it was a ball. Hope would promptly fetch her toys and drop them next to her toy box for Rosanne to pick up and put away. If she was outside and done playing for the day, Rosanne would ask her to collect her babies and bring them in the house, and she would. She would run around the backyard picking up all her toys and depositing them at Rosanne's feet. In fact, she was such a good cleaner that she would clean up not only her toys but also the toys that Murray left behind. She was very fast and very smart.

She also loved to play fetch with her ball. When the family gathered in their back room to watch television, Hope would hand someone her tennis ball so that it could be thrown up and over the upstairs balcony. She would run to the front of the house and up the stairs, locate the ball, and then peek through the railings, showing everyone that she'd found it. It took only a minute before she was back downstairs, tail wagging, and handed off the ball to someone else to repeat her fetch game.

With Mitch, playtime had a whole new meaning. He and Hope had wrestling matches, chased each other around the house, and made laughter sounds that had you laughing along with them, and they would both enter a room with great big grins that made you wonder what they were up to. They were a family now, all of them together, basically for better or for worse. They played rough and tumble but cuddled lovingly each night. For six years it was perfect, until ...

Hope began reacting negatively to the sounds of thunderstorms and normal house sounds like the timer on the stove, test alert warnings from the television, a hair dryer, and even cameras clicking. Little did the family know that issues within her body were causing electrical surges and that sounds once normal were aggravating her internal circuitry.

A Call to Action

I t was Hope's seventh birthday, September 4, and she was surely not acting like herself. She wasn't running around with vigor, and she began requesting to go out for potty more frequently. She occasionally threw up, but that did not alarm her family much. She did this on occasion after indulging in a yard "Tootsie Roll" now and then, a habit she'd continued from her days of searching for food on her own. Veterinary care should be the first place to go when there may be a physical issue with a pet; therefore, on September 6, 2011, Rosanne had to call her vet and get Hope in immediately for an exam. A small red bump that was found on Hope's right hind leg just four days earlier was now a red, raised bump and getting larger. Hope also displayed symptoms of a possible urinary infection.

At the vet's office, Hope's exam consisted of a urinalysis and FNA impression smear from the mass. Both results were completed immediately, and the decision to surgically remove the mass was made and scheduled to be done in three days. The doctor did not seem alarmed, but because of how fast the mass appeared and grew, he believed that it needed to be removed and tested sooner than later. Rosanne agreed without a doubt. On September 9, Hope had her surgery to remove the mass, and the wait for test results of the biopsy began.

On September 19, Hope had her stitches removed and had a quick exam of all her vitals. For that day, she was happy. She began running around a little more, but she still had the urge to go out more than usual. The vet prescribed Proin for urinary incontinency to help Hope with the frequent potty urges and then provided Rosanne with the results on the lump—it was benign. Hope started a round of nose kisses for all with such great news.

But on October 10, another trip to the vet was made, because Hope wasn't using her left leg; she was just toe tapping when she walked. Her vet carefully massaged and examined her leg. He came to the conclusion that she might have pulled a muscle or overextended it while running. His recommendation was to ice the area and try to keep Hope quiet for a few days. While icing wasn't a problem, keeping Hope still was. Hope had many jobs to do at home on a daily basis. She had to keep Murray in his place, protect the house, chase the squirrels in her yard, and bark at the mailman from her spot on the sofa.

But on October 16, just six days after her vet appointment, Hope was outside trying to do her business when a large yelp that would not stop came from her mouth as she fell to the ground on her right side, kicking her hind legs while trying to get back up. Rosanne screamed for her youngest son, Mackenzie—who by this time was commuting to college—to help carry Hope to the car. Once again, Rosanne frantically drove Hope to the local animal emergency clinic to see what was wrong with her baby.

Four hours, six x-rays, and a thorough exam later, the emergency doctor stepped into their room. By this time, Rosanne's husband had arrived and was assisting Hope to walk outside for a potty break. With everyone present, the doctor began. "There is a large sublumbar mass with ventral displacement of the colon." Rosanne's jaw dropped, her eyes began to water, and her skin color lost all shades of pink.

"What did he just say?" she asked as she wrapped her arms tightly around Hope as they sat on the floor together. They were advised that Hope needed to have an ultrasound and biopsy done to determine a final diagnosis.

"I'm sorry," was all the doctor could offer as he sent them home with tramadol for swelling and Deramaxx for pain along with discharge instructions. He sternly advised that they call their vet first thing Monday morning.

On Monday morning, Rosanne's vet, Dr. Jones, called her as soon as they opened. He had received the emergency report and had already made calls for her to get Hope in as soon as possible to a specialist of veterinary internal medicine and oncology in Akron. The tone of his voice was soft, articulate, and concerned. Having known her vet for over nine years, Rosanne could tell that something was not right.

She finally blurted out the question she did not want the answer to. "Does Hope have cancer? Are we able to get rid of it?"

Her vet took a moment with a deep breath and told her that Hope needed to have a few more tests to determine what all was going on inside her. They would discuss her question when they had all the results. In the meantime, he made an appointment for Hope with the specialist for Friday, October 21.

Hope's vet and all who worked with him knew how much Rosanne cared for all animals. He knew she would ask where, how, and when before he called her. The veterinarian office first met Rosanne in the summer of 2002 when she brought in a week-old squirrel that had fallen out of its nest. She had no idea how to care for it and was looking for advice. The office staff took thirty minutes of their time to educate Rosanne on nursing the squirrel and sent her home with mother's milk, a baby bottle, and swaddling. Rosanne left the office cradling the little one, naming it "Baby Hopeful" in the hope that she could keep it alive. After three days with its substitute mother, Baby Hopeful passed away in Rosanne's arms, held close but not alone. The vet's kindness and sincere love for the little squirrel made such a huge impression on Rosanne that she switched from her current vet to them immediately.

Hope's next five days went by with no improvement, but she did not express discomfort, either. October 21 arrived, and a road trip was made to the specialist. The appointment was lengthy. Sometimes Rosanne and her husband were with Hope, and sometimes she was off by herself for tests. All in all, Hope did remarkably well with her demeanor as new people handled her and guided her off to exam rooms. She had two ultrasounds, a full-body exam, a CBC profile (complete blood count), a biochemical profile, and cytology sampling done. Since Hope's first visit to her vet on September 6, she had lost eight pounds, going from sixty-six to fifty-eight pounds. Her appetite decreased, she remained lame, and she had developed difficulty defecating. The specialist entered Hope's room ready to spout off medical terms and procedures when Rosanne stopped her and requested if she would kindly tell them like it was, simply put. The vet specialist began with the mass in Hope's abdomen, but what she said next made Rosanne and her husband shudder.

The tests revealed a three-centimeter anal gland mass along with another mass pressing on her precious dog's colon. *How could this have happened? What sign did I miss these past seven years?* She did not like how the visit was ending. She already had it in her mind that she was going to do anything and everything to help save her Hope. She was not sure how. All she knew was that her husband was okay with whatever decision she made. Rosanne knew that she needed to cut back expenses a lot on whatever she could to pay for Hope's cure. There was no doubt there. They had to wait another five days until all the results were in so that treatment could be discussed.

Rosanne felt at a loss, absolutely powerless. It was as if the weight of the world was on her shoulders. *What am I going to do? How should I proceed?* She became more and more anxious as her mind whirled, immediately searching for the first thing she should do or who to contact for help. She had to do something, and she must be strong for Hope. All she could think of was that her precious baby, whom she'd had for such a short time, may be leaving her.

How will Mitch react? He and Hope are partners in crime. He was such a sensitive, old soul for one so young. He had so much on his plate already with working and college. She couldn't ask him for too much support and help. He had enough to do. "No!" she shouted out loud and stomped her foot. "I will not give up on Hope. I don't care if everyone else sees no future for her. I have her sitting right here next to me, and that's where she's going to stay."

Rosanne turned to look at her beloved dog. Oh, those sweet, tender, trusting brown eyes. They were just staring back at her as if to say *Now what do we do?* It was up to Rosanne to find the way.

This burden was almost too unbearable. She would gladly grant her health to her wonderful dog, but it doesn't work that way in life. Planting a gentle kiss on Hope's nose, she vowed that she would do everything in her power to help her through the medical battle as long as Hope wanted that too.

How will I find out?

Rosanne lifted her eyes to heaven to pray for guidance. *O Lord, please help me know what to do and how to care for Hope. Please send someone to help me*, she prayed with tears in her eyes and pain in her heart. All she could think of was her adorable doggie running happily around the backyard. She smiled at that thought and blinked back her tears. As Rosanne made her way toward her computer desk, her eyes came to rest on something she had posted on her clipboard since October 18, 2009. It had been there so long that she'd never really paid attention to it. *What is this?* She started to read the write-up about an animal communicator extraordinaire. At least that's what the paper said. *I wonder how this works, and what does an animal communicator actually do? I know what Hope wants by her body language. I know when my dog is hurting, when she wants to eat, and when she wants to go out. Is there more to it than that? I bet the animal communicator just reads the pet's body language. Anyone can do that! Well, anyone who is tuned into their pet, that is!* Rosanne certainly knew everything about her dog from their years together, for she was a hands-on pet mom. *Well, what could it hurt?* Any port in a storm!

That very day, October 22 (two years and four days from the date that Rosanne received information of my services), Rosanne called me, the animal whisperer, and said that my services came highly recommended from a mutual friend. Rosanne immediately inquired how animal communication worked and what could it do for her. She explained that her dog Hope was very ill; she never once said *dying*, for that would be like admitting defeat.

I started to explain how the process works. "It's simple," I told her. "You simply provide me with a picture of your pet and a list of questions and issues that you want me to identify for helpful solutions. Then tell me how long you would like me to spend talking to your pet. The fee is one dollar per minute," I explained.

A baffled Rosanne asked, "How does it *really* work?"

"That's easy," I said. "I use telepathy to read or communicate with your dog's mind using images and words to project my questions and to obtain answers."

It was Rosanne's impression that Diane thought this was very simple and a common occurrence, but for her ... wow, she was blown away. *Could a dog truly communicate thoughts? Did this type of thing really exist?* There was dead silence on the phone as Rosanne tried to process my explanation of how it was done.

I continued. "You see, I've been psychic all my life. I have visions and can jump from the present to the past quickly. I talk to the dead all the time. You know, people and animals. I do 'em all, dead or alive," I told her as I laughed.

This was a completely new concept for Rosanne. She had been to mediums and angel card readers. Rosanne's Catholic faith was strong, but she still believed deep down inside that there was some margin of truth to this psychic thing. After all, didn't the Bible mention prophets all the time, and didn't Saint Francis of Assisi talk to the animals? *I guess it could happen,* she thought. *What do I have to lose, anyway?* She quickly stopped questioning herself and said to me, "Okay, let's do this."

I laughed again but then got very serious. "Tell me what you think is wrong with your dog. You've taken her to a vet, right? I'm not a vet—not even a vet tech—but I have a lot of training in energetically healing animals and people. I am a Reiki master, which is the highest level you can go in energy healing for people. Reiki can be used to provide healing to anyone or any pet, no matter where they are located. I mostly perform distance work on pets using a surrogate stuffed animal, because my clients are located all around the United States. Plus, I have taken years of training as a Healing Touch for Animals (HTA) practitioner. I work with Bach Flower essences, tuning forks, aromatherapy, and healing with color. But first, Rosanne, I want you to e-mail me everything the vet told you, plus send me a picture of Hope and any questions you have. We'll go from there."

Now, Rosanne thought, *we have an action plan. Not sure if it's going to help, but it can't get any worse, so Hope and I are going to give it a try.*

Later that day, as I checked my e-mail, and sure enough, there was a message from Rosanne with several pictures of Hope. The first picture was Hope at one and a half years of age. *Oh, my God, this dog is adorable!* Of course, in my eyes, all animals are adorable. I've never met one that I didn't want to kiss and hug.

Okay, now back to reading the e-mail, I chastised myself. *Got to find out what is going on inside that sweet doggie.*

Rosanne e-mailed me on October 23.

Thank you for speaking with me yesterday. My day went a little easier after our conversation. Hope even slept all night without having to go outside. Would you please spend thirty minutes with Hope? I will be with her all day today enjoying lazy time and sunshine. Here is the scoop I have so far. As of our emergency visit to a vet group in Akron on Friday, here is the diagnosis in laymen's terms: There appears to be a very large mass or several severely enlarged lymph nodes in Hope's sublumbar region. Given the presence of the mass in the left anal gland region, they suspect this represents metastatic neoplasia. Samples of the sublumbar mass and lymph nodes were taken for evaluation by a pathologist. The results will return early next week, and they will call with treatment options. They did not take x-rays of her chest, because so far, all other body parts are good with the exception of the gall bladder and the urinary bladder that are both moderately distended. That is because, according to the vet, the mass is pushing everything down. (In other words, if you were to take a picture of Hope down her spine, you can see large, round, shaded egg shapes on either side of her spine right above her hips.) This mass, they say, may or may not be connected to the three-centimeter mass they found in her anal passage. She is carefully using her left hind leg, walking as if a nerve is being pinched because she has no control of the muscle. She walks with her left hind foot out at a slight angle, with toe touching the ground as her guide not to stumble. She lost eight pounds in eight weeks, and her eating has been on and off. Hope did eat well yesterday. We supplemented half her hard food with healthy, filling, softer food, providing meals of meat and veggies. She ate great this morning.

I have many questions to ask Hope.

1. *Are you in pain every day, and where does it hurt?*
2. *Do you know how much I love you and that I'm doing everything possible to improve your well-being?*
3. *What happened about a year ago that has made you afraid of having your picture taken? Would you please have your picture taken with Mitchell and me this week?*
4. *Can you tell me why you growl at Murray, Callie, and Apollo when they affectionately come up to you? Especially Murray after all these years? (Callie and Apollo are her feline family members.)*

I have so many more questions for her, such as who abused her and why she fears beeping alarms, the cooking fan, fireworks, and—this past year—her fear of thunderstorms. Will you please tell her how much we appreciate her protecting us and loving us unconditionally—that we know how smart she is and how wonderful it is that she retrieves and cleans up her toys when we ask? Hope is unbelievable. I have attached multiple pictures. The head shot is her at one and a half years old. However, the last three blurry pictures were taken this morning. This silly dog would not pose for the pictures. The last picture is our other dog Murray, who is in front of Hope. The left side that bothers Hope is facing you. I await your call.

I reviewed the information that Rosanne had sent, and then I brought up the pictures of Hope on my PC. *Ah, what a love,* I thought as I printed out all the information Rosanne had sent me.

Once I had all the information in my hot little hands, the first thing I did was select my favorite picture of Hope. I said my prayers as always before starting my animal communication and asked for all my spirit guides, animal totems, and Saint Francis of Assisi to assist me to obtain a clear communication between the two of us for everyone's highest good. I gazed at Hope's picture. "Hi, Hope. Your mom, Rosanne, would like me to talk with you. I am Diane, and I am your friend and your mom's friend. I would like to talk with you about a few things, because your mom has some questions for you, and she wants me to give you a message. Is that okay with you?" I waited for a response. It only took a second or two for Hope to respond back.

"That would be fine with me," the dog communicated telepathically. I heard her voice in my head.

I told her, "First thing I'd like to do is check your chakras, which are invisible energy wheels inside your body that help regulate your vital organs. I've heard you're not feeling well, and I would like to see if I can help, if that is all right with you?"

"Will it hurt?"

"No, not at all. You won't feel a thing as I check them with my pendulum."

"What is a pendulum?"

"It's a chain or string with something weighted like a crystal hanging on the end that I can use to obtain yes and no answers. I use this tool to determine if your energy wheels or chakras are open or closed. This helps me decide the type of healing I need to perform," I explained.

"Okay, go ahead."

"Thank you very much. Just relax, and I will use a stuffed animal, a sheep, as a surrogate for you. It will only take a minute, and then we can talk." I held my hand on the root chakra of my stuffed animal. The root chakra is located at the junction where the tail meets the animal's body. Eyes fixed on Hope's picture, concentrating on her root chakra, I held the pendulum in my left hand and watched it swing. For me, if the pendulum goes in a perfect circle, the chakra is open, which is good. Anything other than a perfect circle indicates a blockage or physical issue. When other people use pendulums, they may have a different outcome for yes or no answers. It's different for everyone, although my responses are a very common interpretation.

The pendulum started to move horizontally, almost as if it was shaking its head *no*. I made a mental note and went on to the next chakra. At the sacral chakra, which is located about three to four fingers' width from the root, right at the top of the hip, the pendulum again began to move in a horizontal fashion as if to say *no*. Again, I made a mental note and kept going.

The next point of contact is the solar plexus, which is where everyone holds their feelings. On an animal, this chakra is located at the center of the back along the spine. If a person or animal has a blocked solar plexus, it could indicate that they are upset about something emotionally or physically. When humans are upset, they have been heard to say the old adage, "I am so upset, I'm sick over it." That is where the phrase comes from. What it actually refers to is a blockage in their solar plexus. On a human, this chakra is found approximately one inch above the belly button.

Good news—Hope's solar plexus was open and functioning just fine. I blew out a "Whee!" under my breath and kept going. I was worried for a moment that Hope would be completely shut down, and that wouldn't be good.

The next chakra, known as the throat, is found at the back of the animal's head where it meets the body. "Open as well," I muttered. "This is looking good." Then I tried the heart chakra, which is located between the two front legs up into the chest. *Everything good there; it's starting to look more promising,* I thought.

The third eye, or ajna chakra, is located right between the eyes. I moved my hand to the space between the eyes on my stuffed sheep. The pendulum swung in a perfect circle again. *Great!* I was ecstatic with this outcome. *Last one coming up,* I thought as my hand moved to the top of the head on the crown chakra, located between the two ears. Again, it spun in a perfect circle.

Before any healing could begin, I needed to check on the special area every animal has that holds its life force. Other components of this unique area include how they connect to the universe and where their souls are held in the spirit body. The first step is to check the life force. That point is located on the animal's body between two of their chakras, the sacral and solar plexus. I moved my hand to the appropriate location on the stuffed animal, never taking my eyes off the same area on Hope's picture. The pendulum did not move. *Oh, oh no! That is not good at all!* That meant that Hope's will to live was diminished. *Crud!* I tried to push down the panic inside myself. Because I knew about Hope's diagnosis, I realized that she needed her life force to be strong to get her through this illness.

Move on; you're not done yet. Next I checked the soul, and hers was open. My hand moved to the appropriate spot on the stuffed animal while I looked at the same location in Hope's picture. I needed to assess her connection to the universe. Nothing, no movement at all! *Crap, that's blocked too!*

I started to scribble notes on the paper in front of me. "Blocked root, sacral, life force, and her connection to the universe," I wrote. *That is a lot of issues! Better get busy.* I put down my pendulum and started talking to Hope.

"I'm back," I told her. "Before we talk and I tell you what Mom wanted you to know, I have to do some healing on you, okay?"

Hope said, "I knew you would say that. Sure, go ahead. It won't hurt, will it?"

I smiled. *She is such a cute dog.*

"No, not at all, in fact, you will feel very relaxed and at peace. You may get sleepy, and if you want to doze off, you go right ahead. It will feel a little warm as I move my hands energetically on your body, but it will be pleasant, I promise you. It won't hurt in the least. You just lie back, relax, and enjoy it!"

First Healing for Hope

M y mind wandered back to the beginning of my healing career. Throughout my years in the animal communication/ healing business, as I talk to my animal clients, I understood that they needed healing physically or emotionally for many reasons. Some had been abused or abandoned; some were simply physically sick like Hope. I could actually "hear" their cries for help. Determined to help them as best I could, I began to seek out how I could accomplish this goal. It wasn't easy back when I first started my business in 2003. I searched for classes for healing animals but couldn't find any. What I found was Reiki, a Japanese method of healing people. The term represents the Universal Life Energy that is all around us. When you apply Reiki for the purpose of healing, it accelerates the body's ability to heal or repair physical ailments and opens the mind and spirit.

Learning Reiki was not an easy process. It took time, practice, and money. As I was learning, I would repeatedly ask my teachers to tell me how to perform healing on an animal. I would inquire, "If this was an animal, what would I do?"

My teacher laughed and then scolded me. "We are not talking about animals, Diane!" She seemed extremely put out that I would even ask, but another of my teachers whispered, "Do it this way," and she showed me how it was done.

I smiled to myself, thinking back to that time. It was fun and frustrating all at the same time. It felt good learning it, but I needed more. Then, during a class on how to use my animal communication skills in a business environment, I heard about Healing Touch for Animals (HTA). Now *that* was just what I needed.

After years of study and practice as I worked with my animal clients, utilizing Healing Touch became second nature to me. It is my go-to energy healing technique that I use almost daily. I feel that I am really invoking a change in my pet client's energy field when I use HTA. I have witnessed some miraculous physical and emotional changes that reinforce my belief that this holistic energy healing really works well.

When I use HTA, I work with the bioenergy field of the animal's body to promote wellness. HTA provides specific energy techniques and a hands-on application that works on all species of animals. I have found that HTA principles use basic science to maintain and regulate a healthy immune system. The healing modality was created by Carol Komitor, and her mission is to teach and apply energy medicine, assisting animals with their health and well-being while building a deeper connection between animals and humans.

HTA benefits an animal by relaxing the body and muscles, increasing circulation, elevating oxygen levels, assisting with nutrient absorption, regulating hormones, releasing toxins from the body, promoting cell growth, and healing. HTA can help animals with the following issues: injuries, illness, behavioral problems, stress, trauma, surgery and recovery, competition, connection with other animals and humans, and euthanasia.

In both Reiki and HTA, I have learned to perform distance evaluations and healing. This means that I do not need to be in the physical presence of the person or animal in order to determine the areas of his or her body that require healing or to actually perform healing. I can use my skills on a surrogate, like another animal or person, stuffed toy, or even myself. Using distance evaluation and healing is very helpful to me personally. It means that I can energetically review a person or animal at any time of the day or night and perform energy healing on any issues that I find. Travel is not necessary, and sometimes staying at home works in my favor. Animals can get very distracted when a new person visits. This distraction takes away their focus from both telepathically talking and healing them energetically. It is very hard to keep your hands on a dog that is excited, going in circles or hurting. Additionally, most people work outside their home, and syncing our schedules can be cumbersome, to say the least. I have had that experience many times and decided that working from home and using the distance healing is best for me and the animals I work on most of the time. That is not to say that I have not performed many healings in person. Several holistic healing modalities that I use require me to be in the actual presence of the person or animal. Aromatherapy, tuning forks, and healing with crystals and color are techniques that necessitate my physical presence with my client.

Many healing techniques are utilized in both HTA and Reiki. For example, I learned how to repair an animal's life force, soul, and connection to the universe along with their chakras early on in my training. Before I perform a chakra healing, I would need to strengthen the dog's life force. Once her connection to the universe and life force was reestablished, it would provide Hope with a life-sustaining energy system that would give her the greatest potential for healing and also provide emotional stability and a deep connection between her and the universe.

First, I had to determine how these areas were presenting themselves. With one hand on the life force area and the other hand holding my pendulum, I determined that it was so fragmented that it was virtually gone. This was not a good thing.

In people, the life force, or *tan tien,* is located right below the navel. On dogs, their life force is located on their back before the hip area. Our will to live or life force is very important for both people and pets in energy healing. It is the center of our energy and power. I would need to ensure that Hope's was open and moving freely.

After calling in my spirit guides, Jesus, the greatest healer of all, and Saint Francis of Assisi to assist me to provide the best healing for the animal's highest good, I set my intention and using my stuff animal started the energy flowing by placing both my hands on the area where her life force was located. The restorative energy began to flow through me to Hope. Providing the universal healing energy through me to an animal always fills me with love and peace. It feels so comforting to perform, almost like a loving caress. Once I could feel the energy moving under my hand, I lifted one hand away and began to pull life force together, almost like pulling threads to weave a rope. Once it was all gathered, I continued to send healing energy to her life force. As I performed the correct steps, I felt the energy beginning to move appropriately. I could feel her life force under my hands whirling in a clockwise motion, and I could sense her physically perk up. I was ready to work on her soul. The soul is located behind the heart, almost like a support system for that organ; however, the soul is not a vital organ but is the essence or the spirit of an animal or person who chooses to come to earth, allowing him or her free will.

I positioned my hands for this next phase of healing, and when I felt the energy was strong, I brought both my hands together using a different protocol to modulate the energy to the correct place. This protocol is very powerful for me. Whenever I perform it, I can feel the results immediately. My hands feel very hot, and they tingle when I use this healing technique. *Everything is going well,* I thought.

One last area I had to fix was her connection to the universe. Now that her life force and soul were open and functioning correctly, I could move on to the last phase of this protocol. With one of my hands on her soul, I moved my other hand to the appropriate location on my surrogate stuffed animal. I closed my eyes to feel the energy moving. Once I felt that I had a good connection between her soul and the universe, I brought my hands together one last time, using the powerful healing technique I love so well to finalize her healing.

Wow, this was such a powerful healing that I was having a hot flash; performing intense healings always brought on my own personal summers, if you know what I mean. I guess that is an indication for me that I was doing my best for her.

After this part of the protocol was complete, I picked up my pendulum to determine if I was successful in opening all appropriate energy points on Hope. I moved my hand first to the life force, and with my pendulum in my other hand, I watched it start to move. *Nice circle,* I thought. Next I moved my hand to the surrogate sheep's soul and again was rewarded with a perfect circle. *That's what I like to see.* Moving my hand to the area for her connection to the universe, I found that the pendulum swung in a nice round circle moving at a good rate. *Perfect,* I thought.

Now it was time to perform a different healing protocol on Hope's chakras using my surrogate stuffed animal. A fully functioning chakra system will help expand the pet's energy field to allow the energy to freely run through his or her body. This in turn will help to accelerate the healing process.

I set my intention to send energy and healing to Hope's chakras and then started on her root chakra, located where the tail meets her body. I began the protocol, as I was taught years ago, moving my hands after modulating the energy flow. My hands felt very hot, just as they always do when I'm sending the universal energy. I worked with my eyes glued to Hope's picture, closing them only to ensure that I was feeling the particular chakra open before moving on to the next chakra. I continued working on her seven main chakras and then moved on to balance the minor chakras in Hope's legs and hips. Hope took a huge amount of energy. My hands felt like they were on fire. The healing was very intense, but that is normal for me. The entire process is very time consuming but well worth it. After the healing, Hope's chakra system was running like a well-oiled machine.

After all the energy movement, I checked in with my pendulum on my work to her chakras. They were all open and flowing freely. I felt confident that she would be feeling much better and moving with less pain.

Let's Talk

"Hi, Hope. I'm back with you," I telepathically communicated. "How did you like your healing?"

"It was wonderful!" Hope exclaimed. "I almost fell asleep, but I wanted to stay awake to talk with you. It's never happened that I found a human that can actually 'hear' what I have to say. I couldn't possibly miss that!"

"Oh, I am glad about that. Hope, your mom, Rosanne, would like to ask you some questions. Is that okay with you?"

"Yes, I am excited to hear from her."

"First and foremost, your mom wants to know how you are feeling."

"I am in pain, but it is okay. It comes and goes. Some days are better than others. I like the sun; rain makes me sad.

"As far as food goes, I would like the ham to keep coming. It smells fabulous! My sniffer still works. I like the creamy stuff; it's good, too."

Rosanne had told me that she had been wrapping up Hope's medicine in shaved ham to get her to eat it and was praying

30

that she would not notice due to the strong odor of the ham. Obviously, it was working, as Hope was not wise to this tactic. I would not give away her secret.

I told Hope that her mom was very worried about her and loved her very much. She wanted to do everything possible to help her.

"Mom is an angel. She fusses and worries about me. I don't want to make her sad. I will get better. I'm willing to try anything. If I go to the vet, will it hurt? Will I be away for a long time? Will you be with me?"

I reassured Hope that the vet would not hurt her and she would not have to be away from her family for a long period of time. I also told her that Rosanne would go with her to the new vet.

"Why won't you sit still to have your picture taken?" I inquired.

"Picture is scary. Point that machine at me. Afraid it is going to hurt me. Murray said they shoot you. I don't want to be shot."

"Oh, Hope, it's not actually going to shoot you! Murray was just teasing you. A camera will point at everyone, and then someone will click a button on the camera to capture the photo of you with your family," I explained.

"I will sit on Mom's lap. I will try the picture, but I may close my eyes if I am afraid."

I laughed at her response and said, "Why do you growl at Murray?" Rosanne wanted to have an answer to this question.

Hope growled. "I don't want anyone messing with me or my leg. I feel unsteady, so don't knock into me. It hurts. I have to ease myself down. They don't get it! I told them, but they don't think I am serious. I must be strong."

I explained to Hope that her mom appreciated the fact that she protects the family. I complimented her on being so smart and helping out at home as Rosanne requested.

"I would do anything for Mom. She's my girl. She smells pretty and is always nice. She hardly yells and gives me table scrapes to help me eat more."

I thanked Hope for talking with me and told her to remember to be nice and have her picture taken for her mom. Sure enough, when I heard back from Rosanne, Hope had indeed sat on her mom's lap for her picture, and you could even see the Saint Francis medal that she wore. What a beautiful girl!

Hope also was able to join Rosanne in the upstairs of their home after I opened her chakras, which she had not been able to accomplish before her treatment. Rosanne was convinced that angels had sent us to be together. I agreed with her.

In the meantime, Mitch did not take a backseat in finding help, medicine, or a possible cure for Hope. He got on the Internet and searched for everything he could with regard to dogs with cancer. He found many websites, each having their own remedy or suggestions, but he was drawn to the subject of food first, for it would be the quickest and easiest way to start. He read that cottage cheese and flaxseed oil once a day would help ease gas in Hope's abdomen and make it easier for her to defecate. He also read that certain foods were bad for cancer patients, especially white potatoes, and that grain-free seemed to be the consensus for a healthier diet. So Hope's family changed her diet to a more natural and holistic grade of food that was high in fat and grain-free. On October 24, while Mitch was studying for a test in the early hours of the morning, he found a prayer blog online and asked for healing prayers for Hope. He wrote with such perseverance and love that he received many kind notes back personally, and many more people responded by sending their prayers out into the world. One lady particularly sent a link for a remedy of tea. She stated that it had been used by people and dogs with cancer and other issues and that she had personal testimony of its healing properties. The herbal tea contained burdock root for the liver; sheep sorrel for detoxification and swelling; slippery elm to provide a mucilage coating for the throat, mouth, stomach, and intestines; and turkey rhubarb to cleanse the digestive system. *Could this be the miracle?* Mitch thought as he forwarded all the prayers and information to his mom. Rosanne immediately searched online to read all about the tea, along with its background check. She found the ingredients to be all natural and did not hesitate to order the capsules before nightfall.

On October 27, the results were in, and the specialist once again had no positive information. By now, all Rosanne wanted to hear was what she could do to make Hope well. The vet specialist informed her of a doctor willing to undertake the removal surgery but expressed the high risk and vascular and neurological complications that could come about, not knowing the severity of the lymph nodes until they opened Hope up. Rosanne did not think long on this offer, and she graciously declined. This definitely would not improve Hope's quality of life. The doctor then offered radiation with an oncologist in Columbus. The appointment would be one day a week for four to six weeks. Rosanne and Hope would travel to and from Columbus. There was one test that Hope had not had yet, and that was a chest x-ray. If the heart was strong and the cancer had not spread, radiation might be a solution. But this solution was not a cure; it would only give Hope a four- to six-month extension to her life.

Rosanne thanked the vet specialist for her information and told her that she needed to have a family meeting on all the updates. Without hesitation, Rosanne immediately called her vet and was in their office that day for Hope to have a chest x-ray. The roller coaster of emotions was becoming unbearable, and sitting in the waiting room again for results was extremely stressful.

Moments later, Hope's vet called Rosanne into the exam room to view the results. They were far from joyous. The chest cavity had metastasized lymphoma which showed as small multiple spots on her chest x-ray.

Settling In for the Long Haul

Rosanne and I were on speed dial to each other. When we were not talking about Hope's condition and her symptoms, we were plotting to bring in additional help in the form of a holistic vet. Rosanne's son continued web searches for whatever information he could find regarding dogs with cancer. Between the three of us, we printed and pored over many pages of information from the Internet. We were all just trying to find something, anything. We were all looking for a miracle. We learned a lot, and we were informed, but what we found was not promising. However, we were a team. I'm not sure who was leading our team, but I actually believe it was Hope. She was our strength. She wanted to live. That was all we needed to know to be motivated to help her in any way we could. Her spirit never faltered. Why would we?

I used animal communication to check in with Hope twice every day. As with any terminal patient, she had some good days and some bad days. I scanned her chakras every morning and balanced them when it was warranted. Distance healing proved to be the best since both Rosanne and I had full-time jobs. I was able to balance Hope's chakras often, sometimes morning and night. Hope was the ideal patient, cooperating with me 100 percent of the time. She wanted to feel better.

In order to make Hope more peaceful and emotionally prepared for the fight of her life, I made a treatment bottle of Bach Flower Essences to help her along.

Bach Flower Essences are all-natural, diluted solutions made from spring water, an alcohol preservative, and the parts of flowers and plants. They are used to help balance the emotions and bring about a state of balance in people and animals.

Bach Flower Essences are not used to treat physical disease but rather the emotional state of your pet. The essences can be used to help resolve fear and anxiety, anger, grief, and many other emotions. The Bach Flower Essences have worked successfully on people and animals to achieve emotional contentment and to alleviate many emotional burdens.

There are a total of thirty-eight different Bach Flower Essences. Thirty-seven are made from flowers, and one is made from the water of a spring believed to have healing properties. The beauty of these essences is that they do not negatively interact with any medicines, radiation, or chemotherapy. They are safe to use no matter what prescription drugs are in the pet's system.

All of the essences are used to relieve a specific characteristic or emotional state, so in order to select the correct remedies for Hope, I needed to think about the behavior that she was exhibiting and her personality. That information, coupled with the knowledge of what she was going through emotionally, was the key to finding the appropriate essences for her.

Bach Flower Essences can provide assistance to rectify most emotional issues and help your pet become happier and well adjusted. After all, our beloved pets cannot go to a psychologist like we can. They cannot talk out their emotional hurts and concerns (unless they know an animal communicator), but they do feel them.

One of the most well-known essences is called Rescue Remedy. Rescue Remedy is a combination of flower essences created specifically to address stress in emergency or crisis situations. The essences used in this formula help with trauma and shock (star-of-Bethlehem), terror and panic (rockrose), hysteria or loss of control (cherry plum), impatience and agitation (impatiens), and faintness and stunned feelings (clematis).

Rescue Remedy is usually used for emergency situations but can be used for treating chronic conditions when appropriate. It can help after an accident or in any situation that causes extreme anxiety, nervousness, or terror. It is perfect for a rescue/shelter animal who is scared or in shock after being brought to a strange place. I keep a treatment bottle of Rescue Remedy at the animal shelter where I volunteer.

Rescue Remedy often has an immediate calming effect and is safe, gentle, and nontoxic. It may be taken as often as needed without fear of overdosing. Rescue Remedy is the only combination remedy prepared and sold ready-made.

None of the essences should be used as a replacement for veterinary care. They should be used in conjunction with traditional veterinary treatment. Many people use Rescue Remedy to calm their pets before a vet appointment, grooming, or during a thunderstorm. All of the flower essences will help people; therefore, you can take it too.

Bach Flower Essences and Rescue Remedy are usually taken by mouth diluted in spring water. A little goes a long way, because it is not necessary to use them directly from the stock bottle you purchase.

If you wish, when you purchase a stock bottle, you may also buy an empty thirty-milliliter eyedropper bottle to be your treatment bottle. To prepare the treatment bottle for use with your pet or yourself, follow the instructions below:

1. Fill the treatment bottle ¼ full with vegetable glycerin, brandy, or vodka to act as a preservative. If you chose not to use a preservative, you must refrigerate the treatment bottle. (This is what I do since I don't want the pets to taste the alcohol.)
2. Fill the remainder of the bottle with spring water (do not use tap water). Spring water is natural, unlike tap water, which can be loaded with chemicals.
3. Put four drops of your chosen Bach Flower Essence(s) or Rescue Remedy in the treatment bottle. (You may combine six or more essences into one treatment bottle.) This is the bottle that you will use to treat your pet or even yourself.
4. Place four drops of the mixture from the treatment bottle or the stock bottle on your pet's gums or tongue, on a treat or small piece of bread. Alternatively, you may apply the mixture to your pet's paw pads, nose, belly, or the inside of the ears. I recommend taking the essences internally for best results.

With Rescue Remedy, the essence will be quickly absorbed. If you see no improvement in fifteen minutes, give an additional four drops. When I blend other essences to make a unique treatment bottle for a client, I recommend that the drops be given three times per day for a period of at least two weeks. Horses require a large dose of ten to fourteen drops three times per day.

In Hope's situation, I made a treatment bottle with the following essence combination: crab apple (cleanliness), gentian (help with discouragement), gorse (hopelessness), hornbeam (weakness), mustard (depression), oak (preserve in adversity), olive (physical exhaustion), sweet chestnut (physical duress) and wild rose (helps with the will to live). See the additional resource section for a list of other essences.

Doctor P. to the Rescue

Rosanne was looking for another vet to help Hope, someone that would think outside the Western medicine box. That's where I could assist. I met Dr. P. in 2005 while taking my Healing Touch for Animals (HTA) seminars. I have nothing but high praise for this vet. She is a wonderful holistic veterinarian who really cares. She sponsored all the HTA weekend seminars, putting in countless hours throughout the years to coordinate and ensure that those interested in receiving the training and information were well equipped to help animals with this healing modality. That being said, Dr. P. was a very busy, sought-after vet. Getting an appointment with her was not easy, especially as a new patient.

Rosanne was told that she couldn't get an appointment with the doctor until January. But this was November! Rosanne was very frustrated but persevered. The ladies in Dr. P.'s office offered to perform hands on HTA for Hope in order to establish an office/patient relationship. It worked. Hope received her initial appointment with the doctor for the first week in December.

In the meantime, I got busy healing. It was already two months since Hope's first symptom arose. She was limping more and just had a rough night of sleep due to a urinary sensation every forty-five to sixty minutes for six hours. Hope and Rosanne were exhausted and finally fell asleep around 5:15 a.m. The following evening went a little easier; after all, anything would be better than their experience from the night before.

Rosanne realized that she, too, had good and bad days based on what Hope was having, and she did not want to miss a sign or forget important information to pass on to me or Dr. P. (when they finally met with her). She began keeping a daily log of eating times (what Hope ate and how much), medicine/vitamins taken, and introduction of raw or cooked healthy and natural snacks. She also documented positive days, bad days, and how many times and how much Hope defecated beginning November 8. When it seemed like Hope wasn't improving, the weather outside made up for it; the fall of 2011 was unusually warm, and the days were brighter. This provided Hope more time outside to breathe in the fresh air and feel the warmth on her body.

For ten days, Rosanne feared that Hope's cancer was moving quickly through her body. She had noted that her stools were tiny, and some days she didn't have any at all. Rosanne called me with updates and asked if I would ask Hope some more questions. Rosanne wanted to know if Hope could tell me what and how she was feeling—pain, tired, happy, or sad? She also wanted her to know that the cats were only worried about her and asked that she would not get mad or snap at them.

Hope and I talked again. She was not in terrific pain, but she was frustrated that she couldn't walk as well as she used to and that it seemed to be getting harder for her to eliminate. Hope understood why the cats kept poking their noses at her, realizing that she wasn't feeling her best. She said she would try to be more patient with them.

It seemed the nightly healings were working on Hope. Her root chakra was open each morning when I checked, which was a good sign. Her bowel movements were more regular, including the size. (One might feel that talking about poop daily is disgusting, but this was a daily question asked by everyone to keep track of the cancer progression or elimination.)

On November 19, Hope had an exceptional day. She began after breakfast with tossing and squeaking her toy happily, and then she saw a deer and ran from the back of the house to the front window, where she sat on the sofa as still as a sphinx for twenty minutes watching the outdoors. Since Hope's actual appointment with Dr. P. was not until the beginning of December, Hope had her first patient-established HTA healing with one of Dr. P.'s assistants on November 22. She had an intense healing and felt great. As a result of all the healing Hope received, she was able to get up on the sofa to sit, sleep with her family on the bed, was eating like a pig, attempted to go up a huge flight of stairs, and seemed very happy. I told Rosanne to always let me know when she took Hope for HTA sessions at Dr. P.'s office so that I didn't overenergize her and so they could observe how she was normally without any energy assistance.

That evening, Rosanne received a call from Dr. P.'s office advising that they were able to give Hope an appointment with the doctor on December 1. She called me immediately with the great news. We were both ecstatic!

Then, on November 23—the day before Thanksgiving in the early evening—I received a panicky phone call from Rosanne. Hope was having a bad night. She had a fever, her stomach was grumbling, she was crying as if in terrible pain, and she couldn't get comfortable. She noted that Hope had begun having difficulty going to the bathroom earlier that day. I felt that this was obviously a symptom of the cancer pressing on her bowels.

I had just come home from work and was busy mopping the kitchen floor, trying to prepare for all the guests I had coming for Thanksgiving dinner the next day. *Ah, well, there goes that,* I thought. I finished the corner I was working on and told my husband that Hope needed me, and I would be gone for a while. I disappeared into my meditation/healing room to attempt to help Hope.

I connected with Hope and told her not to panic. I asked her to send me what she was feeling. (Yes, I can receive that kind of information—this gift is *amazing.*) I started to feel cramping in my stomach area. I said to Hope, "Okay, I got it. We are going to move this pressure out of us together." Using myself as the surrogate for Hope, I began performing the HTA technique that is used to break up energy blockages or congestion. I kept visualizing our system moving and started to feel the blockage breaking up. I kept doing the technique for approximately twenty minutes. Unfortunately for both Hope and me, breaking up the blockage had a small side effect. I felt like I was going to literally blow my bowels out! I knew Hope was feeling it too. I grabbed the phone and ran to the bathroom all at the same time. As all heck broke loose for me (not pretty), I explained to Rosanne that she needed to get Hope outside fast. I tried not to be too graphic, but I was in *pain!* Suffice it to say that Hope and I bonded that day in a very unusual way—and in a way that I don't want to ever repeat! She had an immediate and successful elimination and was feeling much better. And once I finished with my issues, thanks to Hope, I felt much better too. I guess that's the price you have to pay for results.

Once the family knew Hope was calm and relaxing, they left her to rest while they briefly stepped out to purchase a birthday present for Rosanne's husband. As the family members made their way through a local retail store in search for the shoe department, Rosanne detoured to admire some bracelets at a jewelry counter. The first one she touched had hanging charms of angels on it. She loves items with angels, but her eyes drifted off to another bracelet hanging in the middle of the display. As she untangled the bracelet from the rest, she was able to read the words on the hanging charms: *Love … Hope … Faith … Hope.* Every other charm read *Hope.* She had it on her wrist and paid for so quickly that the clerk couldn't keep up with her on the transaction. *Is this a message from heaven?* she wondered.

The day after Thanksgiving, another inspirational message was presented. While Rosanne and Mitch were standing in a checkout line, Mitch tapped his mom on the shoulder and quietly pointed in front of them at the back of a young girl's sweatshirt. Rosanne began reading the saying as tears started to flow. The last line on the shirt read "Never give up hope." She could not believe what it said and again stayed quiet to what seemed to be a message, and it wasn't her last.

Later that day, Rosanne asked her youngest son, Mackenzie, to please pick up Christmas stamps for her from the post office. She requested either angels or whimsical ornament designs, but when he returned, he presented her with stamps of Madonna and Child. After an unsure look to her son, Rosanne glanced back at the stamps, but this time, she noticed the name of the artist underneath the portrait: *Raphael.* Rosanne turned her back to her son as her eyes filled with tears, and she beamed an approving smile. At that moment, she believed she was given a sign by Archangel Raphael letting her know that he was present and that her prayers were received. She felt sure that the prayers she recited daily with Hope by her side had been heard. Rosanne plopped down on the floor next to Hope and wrapped her arms around her, kissing her on the head while whispering into her beautiful ears that their prayers were being heard.

For the next couple of days, Hope started to display a regular bathroom routine. Hope would grumble, and Rosanne would check her nose to see if it was hot or cold. A hot nose indicated that she had to go outside. Rosanne would encourage her to go out regularly so that we wouldn't end up with another episode like the one before Thanksgiving, and she expressed daily to Hope how important it was to please keep her root chakra open to help her eliminate every day. It was working! Hope also had another positive accomplishment of scratching an itch with not only her workable back leg but with her bad leg. She continually attempted to walk upstairs and even enjoyed playtime outside on November 30 running, eating snow and loving it all.

Hope's first visit to Dr. P.'s was rough. She growled and bared her teeth and was disagreeable to the doctor, but the doctor was very calm and patient with her. She could sense Hope's fear and protection of Rosanne. During the session, Dr. P. provided techniques for Rosanne to capture Hope's attention with eye-tracking exercises. When Hope would look at Rosanne, she created more energy outside herself, which was very good for her. They were hoping this technique would help Hope out of her sluggishness. When I asked how it worked, Rosanne explained holding a treat between her fingers so that Hope's eyes would follow the movement of her hand to her forehead and hopefully focus on where the treat was held.

Of course, Hope wasn't too cooperative at the beginning and would walk away with her head down. Rosanne was upset, because she wanted to help Hope so much, but she couldn't get her attention. I wanted to help Rosanne with this task and could see the benefit in the action Dr. P. was trying to get Hope to display. I talked with Hope and explained what Rosanne was trying to accomplish. Hope mistakenly thought the raised hand was a reprimand of some kind. Since we didn't really know what her life was like before she came to Rosanne's family, this was expected. Dr. P. felt that obtaining Hope's attention would help Hope focus. After our discussion, Hope responded positively to the technique with Rosanne.

Hope's second visit with Dr. P. went much better. There was no growling or showing of teeth, which made Rosanne very happy. I'm sure the doctor was relieved too. Dr. P. worked with Hope for ninety minutes. She found that Hope had a yeast infection in her left ear and on each of her front elbows. She also addressed Hope's recent development of burping. Rosanne was told to decrease the intake of cottage cheese she was feeding Hope and instead add a small scoop of plain yogurt or pureed pumpkin to her hard food once a day. This was to calm Hope's stomach since her food was not agreeing with her. Rosanne was also told that the toxins in Hope's body from having anesthesia in October, along with the physical and emotional trauma that came from her past surgery, was finally gone from her system. Hope's body would hopefully respond to the new regimen of natural vitamins now to cleanse and support, provide nutrients, and assist with pain management.

Throughout the appointment, Dr. P. used a spray bottle containing color essences on Hope, which works on a vibrational level to elicit some form of change (balancing and grounding). Rosanne tried to explain and describe to me what the vet was spraying over Hope before and during the appointment. I realized what she was describing was color therapy in the form of Rainbow Spray that I had purchased from Dr. P.'s office in the past. (Dr. P. utilizes a whole line of color sprays for different ailments in her vet practice.) I had used these color essences myself in my animal communication/healing business and loved the outcome. I found that most animals really respond well to them and that Hope really liked them too. The manufacturing company is called AnimalLights, and they have a whole line of colors for different scenarios.

After the healing Dr. P. provided, it was not necessary for Hope to keep her upcoming appointment for HTA at her office. Instead, Rosanne was told about the benefits of imagery, and she was encouraged to use either visualizing or photos posted around Hope's lounging area in the house. She was taught how to visualize Hope being calm and relaxed along with a healing imagery of the tumors shrinking. Once home, Rosanne found a photo of a healthy, internal view of a dog, and she taped it on the wall next to Hope's bed. That evening, Hope had remarkable progress of sitting nice and square and was walking beautifully with the use of three fully functional legs and a left leg toe-tap to guide her steps.

A Christmas Miracle

E very day was a gift, and we all knew it. I, too, celebrated Hope's little victories along with the family. We were in constant contact with each other. I felt I had become part of their family as I went through this struggle with them.

Rosanne and I both knew that the daily energy sent each evening and monitoring of Hope's chakras were extremely important and beneficial for her. This became routine for me, almost like brushing my teeth; however, it was not easy. I had a full-time job, my animal communication business to continue, a family, dog, cat, and horse to care for, as well as all the work I was doing with Hope. I slept less and healed more. I think, in a way, God knew what I was doing and approved, because I always managed to keep everyone happy and get it all done seamlessly. My energy was boundless, probably because of all the healing I was sending through me. When I perform healing on someone else, I receive healing too.

I truly believe the way was divinely paved for me to accomplish all I did, including preparation for the Christmas holiday season.

I knew in my heart that helping Hope and this family was a test of sorts. I think my guides and the angels wanted to see if I had enough courage to do this type of work. I've always been a wimp when it came to animals. I couldn't watch if they were injured or if they passed away on TV. I would feel a piercing pain to my heart as if I had been stabbed. I still feel that way when I see an animal's body on the side of the road, an obvious victim of a car accident. If I could get through this with Hope, I could conquer anything. My emotions were on a roller coaster, as were Rosanne's and those of her family. When Hope had a bad day, I felt it just as they did.

At this point, I realized that Hope would benefit from hands-on daily energy healing. I explained to Rosanne that someone did not need to be born with a healing gene; it was just the desire to perform the healing out of love that made a person a good Reiki healer. Rosanne sure did love Hope. It seemed to me that this would be a perfect solution and would help Rosanne feel empowered to help her dog in a very physical and spiritual way. I arranged for a friend of mine to give Reiki level-one training to Rosanne after the first of the year since the holidays were upon us.

I was blessed that I did not have the day-to-day care that the family was providing to ensure Hope's comfort. It was a lot of work for them. Taking care of a terminally ill animal is much like caring for an ill human. Animals have the same basic needs to eat, drink, sleep, rest, and go to the bathroom. As with the insurmountable challenges human hospice puts on the caregivers, so Rosanne's family found that Hope's needs came before those of everyone else. Rosanne barely slept at night.

The month of December was the month of hope. Each family member wished and prayed for a Christmas miracle of their beloved pet to beat the odds of cancer and for her to be with them at Christmas. Immediately after Thanksgiving, they purchased and put up their live Christmas tree so that Hope could be distracted by its presence. The family knew that the tree brought playfulness and mystery for Hope and that she was aware that soon there would be surprises of goodies under it for her to open, squeak, and of course eat. Her excitement level around the tree was like a kid's in a candy store. The family cats, along with Hope, would all rest around and under the tree in anticipation. In the meantime, trying to figure out what food was best for Hope or what she could eat that would easily digest and provide the nutrients she needed became a health and wellness research project.

One of the in-depth topics of discussion that Dr. P. had with Rosanne was the balancing of daily protein along with benefits of Hope consuming animal organs to provide nutrients for her own organs. Up to this point, the only change to Hope's diet was from a well-known hard dog food bought at a local grocery store to a grain-free product from a pet store that cost double the price. In order to make meal time easier with Hope's new diet, her companion Murray was given no choice, and both dogs began the new feeding regimen together. Before her illness, Hope used to eat three cups of dog food a day and, with her high energy, would keep herself slender at sixty-five pounds. Now her intake of hard food was half a cup twice daily with moist food products added to help her digestion. The goal was to maintain her weight along with providing ease for her to defecate. In addition to adding natural food to her diet, it was important to try to keep it all grain-free as much as possible. She was given cooked chicken liver; gizzards or hearts; sweet potatoes; canned, all-natural pumpkin; tripe; plain yogurt; ground turkey; scrambled eggs without milk; and occasionally a grain-free meal of prepared food from a can. Along with the change in Hope's meals, she was given daily small amounts of flaxseed oil and slippery elm to soften her bowels to make excretion easier.

Up to then, her bodily function and ability to defecate was the most important daily sign of how Hope's day was going to be. If she was able to produce twice a day, the family knew the cancer was quiet. Hope would ask for small walks, and she would run lightly, toss and play with her toy outside, jump up on the sofa to cuddle, or even walk upstairs and lie by Rosanne while she worked at her desk. If she produced pea-size pebbles or liquid gold as a bowel movement, it was a sign that her root chakra was blocked, and the cancer was not giving in. On days when there were changes, Rosanne would contact me after dinner to provide me with updates. It was those updates that would determine the intensity of Hope's need for energy and healing for that evening. For every call made with specific concerns, I would receive an electronic update within forty-eight hours from Rosanne keeping me apprised of how Hope's body responded to her healing.

Through all the ups and downs, tears and smiles, there was only one gift that meant the world to this family, and you could tell by the tone of her e-mail that Rosanne was breathing a little easier knowing Christmas was a week away.

"I thank you again for all your love and time you have put into Hope. My wish has come true. She will be with us this Christmas."

Hope knew how to smile and enjoy life with her family, but she also knew how to look fierce to a stranger. It wasn't until early 2011 that Hope began to show fear both in body language and facial expressions during a thunderstorm, alarms, cameras flashing, and anything that beeped. She was always so brave, so strong, and of course, so beautiful. So when Hope began the fight of her life, every day, Rosanne would lovingly hold Hope's face gently in her hands while they looked at each other deeply through the souls of their eyes, and she would whisper to her, "Please always remember that Mommy loves you, that you are so beautiful, so brave, and so strong." Rosanne wanted to believe that love could conquer all and that by repeating these words to Hope daily, she would create a healing of good against evil within Hope's body to eliminate the cancer. She was not going to give up the fight as long as Hope continued to show a quality of life for herself.

December 23 brought on another set of problems. Normally, Hope was able to accomplish daily cleaning of herself by sitting and curling under, and her family saw this as a physical improvement; however, Hope was hiding the fact that she began leaking again. *How long had this been going on?* Rosanne feared.

The family decided that they were going to forget just for one day, Christmas, the ugly side of cancer, and they were all going to live the day with faith, hope, and lots of love. Hope was so happy Christmas morning, waking each family member with kisses, tail wagging with excitement and trying to get everyone up to see what was under the tree. She could not wait for her slow-moving family to hand out presents, so she decided to grab a gift from under the tree and lie down on top of it to claim it as hers. As the family finally gathered at the tree with all the other animals, Mitch's little helper, Hope, had no interest in passing out gifts. Instead, without waiting any longer, she grabbed the gift out from under her and opened her own present. But how did she know it was really hers? This was truly a gift that kept giving. There were no words spoken for that moment, just lots of teary eyes and great big smiles.

Over the next several days, Hope began to eat less, needing a little assistance with creative feeding, and her left ear began to bother her. She voiced discomfort in a grumble when she moved around, and her stomach sounded off too. Her nose constantly changed from warm to extreme cold, and she displayed shortness of breath just walking in and out of the house or trying to jump up onto the sofa. As quickly as her bad days rolled in, Hope would have another run of very good days. Just days before the New Year, Hope's fever disappeared, her stomach was silent, and she was doing her business effortlessly. She lifted her upper body up to place her front paws on the bed to be petted, walked a quarter of a mile, and walked up the long grade of stairs to be with Rosanne. As every roller coaster slowly moves upward, providing an emotional feeling of suspense or excitement, there is a downside that the rider experiences as either thrill or fear. Well, that was exactly what Hope was experiencing.

Every day, Hope's family watched for some type of physical improvement. Even the littlest display of rolling and wiggling in the snow was monumental. In fact, on January 3, 2012, Rosanne sent me an electronic picture where Hope dropped, wiggled, and rolled in the snow, and it looked like she had made a snow angel. I was amazed at how much it really looked like an angel. This dog was indeed blessed and watched over. This in itself was a miracle, since she previously could barely move. The remainder of her electronic message to me stated that Hope had been displaying wonderful strength and was using her left side. On the flip side, she had some gagging, she made loud, scary noises when clearing her throat, and she was out of breath every once in a while. She was still very happy and had a beautiful outlook on life. It seemed all was good.

Rosanne asked me to check Hope's chest (heart) and throat when I checked her chakra, as I had been concentrating on her hind area. She also noted to me that she'd placed a call to Dr. P.'s office to see if she could get Hope in for an earlier appointment other than the eighteenth due to the gagging issues. In the meantime, Rosanne was looking forward to her initiation into Reiki in February. She enrolled in a college course at

Diane Weinmann

Cuyahoga Community College beginning in January for medical terminology. She believed the more she knew of how the body worked (human or animal), the better she could address Hope's needs.

How are You Feeling, Hope?

T he next e-mail I received from Rosanne was not good news.
She wrote:

It has come to where Hope is uncomfortable. Not all of
the time, but when she is, she really is bad. I could use
a little guidance. Would you please talk with Hope to
find out how much pain she is in (hopefully very little,
just uncomfortable and maybe due to the arthritis in her
back hip is my hopeful wishing)? I need to know if she is
enjoying the food she is eating and if there is a problem
swallowing these days. She has been gagging or clearing
her throat quite often. I feel that I am getting a message
from her that something isn't right, but I don't know
what. She grumbles a lot at night, and she has begun
going tinkle outside at least twice during the night. She
has also made it known that when I am home, I need
to be in her sight. Oh, and can you ask her if she has a
tight chest or problems breathing? I want to make sure I

can inform Dr. P. so we can provide her with something to relieve any pain sooner than later. On a good note, Hope went to have her nails done yesterday. She walks 1/4 mile about three times a week. She has been eating well (sometimes with me coaxing) and prays with me every morning like clockwork.

On February 1, Rosanne told me that she'd decorated her family's full-shaped, beautiful-smelling Christmas tree into a Valentine's Day tree. After all, it had new pine growth, so why throw it out? She then rearranged it on February 19 for Mardi Gras. It was the family tree that kept on giving! As long as the tree had new growth and was rooting from the bottom, she decided she would keep it in the house as a sign of rebirth. For this tree to be cut down in November and still be able to continue to grow was in a way a miracle; therefore, maybe this meant that Hope was being given the same chance. They could both be miracles.

I decided before I talked to Hope that I would check her chakras to see if anything was blocked. Her chakras were all open and flowing freely, and her life force was in place and spinning nicely. This was a good report I could provide to Rosanne, and based on what she'd been through, I was happy to give this information to her. After jotting down these details, I called upon my spirit guides and animal totems to ensure that I received a clear communication for the highest good of all, and then I asked Hope if it was a good time to talk. After receiving her okay, I began our conversation.

I told Hope, "Mom wanted me to talk to you again to see how you are feeling. Can you tell me if you are in any pain?"

Hope replied immediately, "The temperature changes cause pain inside me. I feel achy but not sick."

"How do you like your food? I know Mom has been changing it up a bit."

"The food is good. I like the broth liquid, and it's softer for me to eat."

"Why do you gag?" I showed her what I meant by making myself gag a little.

"My throat tightens when the food is going down, and I panic a bit. I worry I can't get it down and try to cough it up. It doesn't hurt. I can breathe okay."

"All right. Just eat slowly, and try to remain calm. So I hear you are going for walks. Do you like that?"

"Yes, I like my walks very much. I like it outside. I am waiting for the sun. Mom is so kind to me. Tell her not to fuss so much. I won't break! I love them all. Well, the cat is iffy sometimes."

"Anything else you want to tell me?"

"Mom is a good cook. The boy is not bad, either. He sneaks me treats. My nose tickles, and then I sneeze. I liked it at the place where they played with my paws. Sometimes I can put weight on my leg, and it feels better, but that is not too often. I can't do stairs."

"My, you do have a lot to tell me today! I'm going to stop talking now, because I want to send you some healing. Is that all right with you?"

"Sure. I like the healing. It feels so nice, and I get sleepy."

"Okay, just lie down and enjoy, and I'll talk to you again soon," I told Hope.

I called in my healing guides and proceeded to send the universal Reiki energy to Hope using my surrogate stuffed animal. I love giving Reiki. Sending Reiki calms me and seems to put me in a place of peace and tranquility. I certainly hope it does the same for the dog. I knew it would. I've received Reiki many times during Reiki healing shares that I participated in once per month. During those Reiki shares, anyone could come into the local wellness center and receive Reiki free. My friends and I have worked on cancer patients, people in wheelchairs, folks that have recently lost loved ones, and all different kinds of ailments. All of the people were very grateful for the healing they received. In the winter months, we didn't have a lot of people come out for the Reiki share, since it was in the evening; therefore, we'd work on each other. That was heavenly!

Reiki for Rosanne

A s I talked to Rosanne frequently about the many healing
techniques that I use and spoke a great deal about Reiki
(since it was easy to learn, and teachers were readily available),
Rosanne said, "I know what Reiki is and the many reasons for
its use." She understood that it was my way of always explaining
to her how beneficial it would be for Hope (and all animals, no
matter what stage of life they were in), and that convinced her
that she needed to learn it. In an e-mail on December 2, Rosanne
wrote:

> My mind is engulfed in a whirlwind. Long term, Reiki
> will be extremely beneficial for Hope. With that being
> said, I am inquiring about who, what, and where I can be
> trained as a Reiki healer. Is this something that you have
> to be gifted with from God instead of learning? Please
> advise me, as I have a lot of signs and mixed messages that
> I am receiving, and I'm trying to sort it all out.

I told her the next day, "I have lots of friends who could teach you Reiki. No, you do not have to be born with it." I let her know that she could learn it easily, and it's all about the love. I mentioned that I would teach her a little about how to heal the animals, but it was my friend who would perform the Reiki attunements on her that would enable her to bring the energy in to provide healing to herself and others, including her pets.

I talked to one of my favorite Reiki teachers to get her to buy into teaching a level-one Reiki class. Once I had her agreement, I called Rosanne to talk through the arrangements for her to learn Reiki. When Rosanne first asked to learn Reiki, I could think of no one better to guide her on her healing journey of love than my friend Bonnie. Bonnie is a Reiki master. In Reiki, you must hold the master level, the highest level, in order to teach the technique. Although I am a Reiki master too, I have chosen not to teach it, as my focus is more animal communication and healing, not teaching. Bonnie initiated me to be a Reiki master. Her energy is incredible, and her gift to the world is healing where she gives all she can to the cause. She is the gentlest, most loving person I know. I have had the pleasure and honor to work side by side with her performing Reiki healing on many individuals for various causes like breast cancer and MS fund-raising. Working in tandem with her when we perform healing on a person is a true spiritual moment. We almost work as one, together yet apart as we move through our healing routine. Rosanne was in for a real treat.

I arranged for Rosanne's Reiki one training class to be held at my home on February 18. Rosanne wrote:

I'm looking forward to my initiation into Reiki. I was given a book on Reiki for animals to enlighten my mind and soul for the gift. Thank you as always and forever for the love and healing touch you have given and continue to give my girl, Hope. We are extremely blessed to have made a connection with you. I was so excited when you came up with a date for the attunement that I found an animal Reiki book on how to use energy to heal the animals in your life. I read it with lots of note-taking so that I would be prepared and understand any terms or direction that would be given to me. I had found a passage in the book that I had to keep reminding myself of while I was moving forward in providing Reiki for Hope. *As Reiki practitioners, we always remember that Reiki does the healing, and we are only the conduits for this remarkable healing energy. Of course, the fact that we are present and have the intention of bringing healing is an important part of the process, but it is not our own power that does the healing. Although we may have the best intentions for dramatic cures for every problem, healing does not always mean cure. In retrospect, we can usually see how Reiki brought the healing where it was needed the most for the highest good of all.* I had to keep reminding myself that you were providing Hope with a quality of life, just as you would tell me every other time we would talk, but it was so hard moving forward to make decisions in my mind when it was my broken heart that was screaming, "Why, oh, why wasn't she receiving a miracle of being cured?"

Finally, the training day arrived, and Rosanne was really nervous. She told me, "I was afraid that I wouldn't understand what was being taught to me and that I wouldn't be accepted to receive the attunement." Bonnie seemed a little nervous when she got to my house and began to set up her materials. She is such a quiet person that teaching was not something that she aspired to do. I simply thrust it upon her. I'm such a good friend—ha! Hey, I just wanted Rosanne to have the best experience with the best teacher, and naturally, that was Bonnie! Bonnie arranged her books, notes, and pads with pens on my dining room table. I warned my family to keep the noise to a minimum. They are not used to curtailing their antics, so this could be a treat for us all. I was worried. Needless to say, my family was wonderful through the entire day and allowed Bonnie to concentrate on the subject at hand.

I set up a massage table in our living room in order for Bonnie to demonstrate the hand placement for the various Reiki steps in a healing treatment. First came the book work as Bonnie reviewed Reiki's origins and provided general information about the healing modality. This part of the class may seem a little dry for those who prefer hands-on teaching, but it is an extremely important and necessary part of the class. You must have the background information in order to understand the fundamentals that are demonstrated later. Bonnie explained that Reiki is the life force and energy that radiates from a person or animal. It is the air, energy, wind, breath, vital essence—in other words, the activating energy of the universe. Rosanne was very quiet, absorbing all the information, and she took a lot of notes.

Now it was time for the fun to begin, but first, Rosanne had to have an attunement into the Reiki healing modality. When teaching the energy of Reiki, a person is attuned as a Reiki healer, causing their body's energy channels to be opened and cleared of any obstructions. Although everything in life has energy, a Reiki attunement connects the recipient of the attunement to the limitless source of the universe's energy. Attunements are what differentiate Reiki apart from any other hands-on healing modality. The belief is that it actually creates the healer. An attunement is performed with reverence for the ancient teachings of the past. It can actually take a few weeks for someone to adjust to the healing energy after an attunement. After an attunement, you may experience tingling or feel spacey, and you may have diarrhea, a runny nose, or increased urination. It's not like you actually get sick; you are just adjusting to the energy and your ability to channel it. When I was attuned, I felt very light-headed, and I seemed to fly in the air. Whee, frequent-flier miles for everyone!

For this part of the class, I led both Bonnie and Rosanne up to my bedroom where I had a chair in place in the center of the room for the procedure. I discreetly slipped out the door and left them alone for the attunement to begin.

Once I left, Bonnie asked Rosanne a few questions, and then Bonnie requested that Rosanne take a deep breath, clear her mind, and close her eyes. Bonnie put her hand in Rosanne's hand and told her to focus on an image. Rosanne said she recalls feeling weightless as she was imagining Hope running and happy, and she no longer heard the music that was quietly playing in the background (as if she were somewhere else). What she recalls the most was a feeling of air on her face then seeing a full-bodied, white, glowing angel in the distance of her vision. When Bonnie said she could open her eyes, Rosanne had tears trickling down the side of her face. She was all smiles and gave Bonnie a huge hug.

Now for more fun! Bonnie took Rosanne down to the massage table I had set up in my living room. I had sheets and a pillow on the table, just like you would if you were providing a healing session to a client. I was the test client. I love receiving Reiki, so I was excited to jump up on the table and relax. "Do me!" I said, laughing. Bonnie and Rosanne smiled and laughed at my antics, but then we all settled down to business.

Reiki is taught and given with love and reverence if it is done correctly. After giving a silent prayer, Bonnie began with my head and showed Rosanne the specific hand placements, and then she moved on to my chest, down my body, arms, and legs to my feet. You don't need to turn over with Reiki; therefore, I was comfortably resting on my back. It was so wonderful that I almost fell asleep. That is a common side effect of Reiki. When my husband is sick and I provide Reiki healing to him, he usually starts snoring.

The class itself began at 1:00 p.m. and was to end at 4:00 p.m., but with questions, hands-on experience, and catching up on Hope's condition, we were still talking at 6:00 p.m. Rosanne told me later that she felt we were all so kind and welcoming. She said, "I could not wait to get home and try my new gift on Hope." Unfortunately, she told me that she felt like she was all thumbs when she got home, trying to lay out her papers, remembering what to do, and attempting to keep Hope still. She decided to wait until the following evening.

That next day, she was able to provide thirty minutes of Reiki to Hope, and she seemed so surprised. She told me that Hope kept staring at her as if to say, "Is that coming from you? What are you doing?" She laughed and said that it took her an hour before her first attempt to lay out the papers, practice where the chakras were on Hope, and perform the hand movements. She practiced removing the bad energy and sending it off to the universe—a little trick I taught her—never to return again. She did well and was darn proud of herself, and I wholeheartedly agreed.

Rosanne reported to me that for a week, all was going well. Hope would lie comfortably with her for healing for approximately twenty to thirty minutes daily. On February 24, Hope began a gagging reflex all day and every day from that point on. Rosanne told me that one of her most memorable times with Hope was her "Mommy-and-me time" that no one was able to be a part of. Rosanne felt a miracle happened when she saw Hope wag her tail just four days after concentrating Reiki healing energy on her root and tail area. Hope had previously lost the use of her tail around February 12 when she could no longer lift it or wag it. On March 1, another high point was reached when she was able to get up on the futon to take a nap. The constant hands-on healing, given with all the love Rosanne had in her heart, really helped the quality of Hope's life.

Hope on Mom's bed

Hope taking a rest

Hope being silly

Hope in the picture she agreed to take

Hope catching some rays

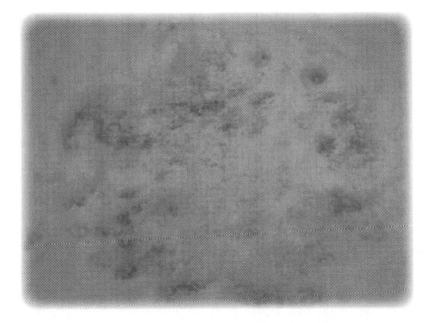

Hope's snow angel

Faith as a puppy

Faith enjoying her toy

Faith in back yard with chew toy

Diane and Faith sharing a kiss

All on Board

The last visit with Dr. P. was on February 23. Hope and Rosanne were there for ninety minutes while Dr. P. performed veterinary contact reflex analysis (VCRA). VCRA is an applied kinesiology method that reliably allows the practitioner to use electrical/electromagnetic interactions of the body to determine the root cause of disease imbalance. The doctor used her index finger as the testing muscle, with her hand on the animal. She gently pushed down on her finger to determine weaknesses and strengths. She also accessed appropriate supplements and dosages, allergens, and emotional issues with this technique.

Dr. P. also performed craniosacral therapy (focused), emotional release / energy work, and a progress health exam on Hope. After the session, Rosanne had a gut feeling that this might be the last appointment with Dr. P. It was noticeably becoming harder and harder to help Hope in the car and make the forty-five-minute journey to her office.

When I asked Rosanne what Dr. P. prescribed, she told me, "Hope was given arnica for inflammation and pain relief." This is a natural pill that humans take, and it works great. This was a switch to remove tramadol out of Hope's system. Between giving Hope Wobenzym—which are digestive enzymes given between meals to reduce inflammation—and arnica for pain, I can attest that they provided the needed relief while Hope was able to be the boss of her body. Hope never showed pain other than toward the end when trying to eliminate her stool.

Beginning February 24, more symptoms started to surface that never seemed to get better. Rosanne called and said, "Hope constantly tried to remove something from her throat; if she stood up, she would spit up small amounts of liquid on the floor; her stools were very inconsistent (squishy, size of small Tootsie Rolls to pebbles to pouring out watery). Then on February 25, Hope's stool was solid twice in one day! I took that as a very good sign. She also tried to wag her tail." Rosanne was very happy, but it was short lived. She told me, "It was very disheartening when our neighbor behind our house let her dog out the same time I let Hope out, and she attempted to run. I caught up to her so that she wouldn't hurt herself, but it was too late; her left leg went extremely limp and unusable. It seemed her burst of energy was too much for her leg to handle, and I provided thirty minutes of Reiki at night in order to ensure that she could sleep comfortably all night. That Reiki training is sure coming in handy."

On February 28, Rosanne e-mailed me to say she found a black spot on the underside of Hope's tail. It felt very hot and had red skin all around it. Additionally, Hope's back right hind leg became extremely swollen. Rosanne provided ten minutes of Reiki to Hope, but Hope seemed extremely irritated, so Rosanne stopped.

Rosanne took care of everyone and everything in her home, including the family-cut Christmas tree, which had been up since November. In January, after she gave the tree granular fertilizer that you would normally use on outside plants, she noticed that the tree started to develop roots. Hope loved the tree so much that Rosanne refused to take it down. Now the tree began to shed, and the brightly green new pine growth began to droop. She took this as a sign that the end was coming.

On February 29, Hope went everywhere Rosanne went, following her even to the point of trying to walk upstairs. She had to hurt; we all knew this. In addition, this was the first day she'd showed that it was getting hard for her to stand up. She just kept on trying until she achieved her goal. We all admired her determination. Rosanne told me that she was only able to provide ten minutes of Reiki, because Hope was agitated again and wouldn't lie still.

By the first of March, Hope was finally able to eliminate a stool that had some substance to it, the first in three days. Her stool had become squishy and orange colored but formed three small plops. She continued to eat well and in the evening was lying on the floor with her family, chewing on her bone, displaying a serene, happy face. Hope was provided with forty minutes of Reiki, and in no time at all, Rosanne found her up on the futon sleeping in her normal position as if she were not ill. All Rosanne could do was stare at her and cry. Hope was indeed a remarkable dog. She was not going to give up!

The next day, she woke up happy and chewed her bone. Still following routine, she conducted her business slowly and methodically, and the end results were two small, very goopy stools. Later that same morning, they changed to fluorescent-gold, phlegm-coated stools. That evening, once again, there yet was another change in her stool condition, but at least she was able to go. With Hope's stool consistency changing constantly, Rosanne was vigilant in her observations. Rosanne noted all this information in the journal she kept to monitor Hope's day-by-day condition. Her morning and dinner feedings must have been tasty, for Hope ate approximately three-fourths of each meal.

The day did not disappoint Hope when it came to the weather outside. It felt and looked like early summer instead of early March. Hope took every advantage to lie around and soak in the warmth of the sunrays through the back room patio doors while once again enjoying her chew bone. Later that evening, she was given twenty minutes of Reiki, as it seemed that was all she wanted.

Healing Hope Holistically

O n March 3, I arranged with Rosanne to visit Hope to perform hands-on healing using both Reiki and Healing Touch for Animals (HTA) techniques, along with my other healing modalities that I practiced. Hope had such a good response from her previous hands-on healing at Dr. P.'s office that we thought this may help significantly in her quality of life. In addition, many of the holistic healing modalities that I use require hands-on service.

I thought back to my first home visit with Hope, which was very memorable. Rosanne kept a tight leash on Hope since Hope didn't like strangers. I started quietly talking to Hope right away, sensing that she would recognize my voice and speech pattern from when I'd talked to her so many times telepathically. It did help somewhat, but Hope was in physical pain and still distrustful of people and their unique smells, so initially I received a low growl from her. I was not to be deterred. Growling did not frighten me. Lucky me, I know no fear when it comes to animals. It helps that I have never been bitten, stung, or in any way hurt by an animal other than my horse accidentally stepping on my foot twice. Even when those incidents happened, I was not injured.

After our initial greeting, we allowed Hope to smell me as I talked to both her and Rosanne. We decided that performing the healing on the floor would be best for all. Rosanne cuddled on the floor with Hope halfway on her lap, holding her head away from me in case she decided to bite. I tentatively placed my hand on her root chakra and, using my pendulum, determined that it was blocked. I progressed one by one, checking all her chakras to enable me to have the big picture of what she was experiencing energetically before starting my healing.

Once my initial evaluation was complete, I began my healing by setting my intention to provide health-giving energy for Hope's highest good and calling in all my spirit guides, Jesus, saints, and angels. This is the normal routine I perform before starting any healing. I placed my hands on Hope in the first location I would work on while Rosanne comforted and occupied Hope with light hand brushing around her neck and face. Hope seemed okay with what I was doing and looked at me and then back to Rosanne. I heard her think that she remembered this happening before at Dr. P.'s office. *Good*, I thought, *she remembers this as a nice experience and will stay quiet as I move through my healing protocols*. I noticed that Hope was taking a great deal of energy, and my hands were extremely hot. That's how I knew it was working. This was good, but due to my age, I started having a hot flash. *Ah, well*, I thought. *Burning up for Hope is the least I can do*. I continued to channel the energy through my hands. I was able to completely perform the technique to balance her chakras, and I could tell by her reaction that she was feeling the energy.

When you provide the universal healing energy to people and pets, many times they become very relaxed and sleepy. Hope was definitely more relaxed and snoozing in Rosanne's lap. I moved on to providing the healing energy to her hips one at a time. I knew it would be very helpful because of her issues standing and walking. Again, she took a great deal of energy, as my hands and heart felt very full. I repeatedly asked for more power, for the angels and both my spirit guides and hers to heal Hope for her highest good. I moved on to healing her back legs. She was still enjoying the energy and was not moving. *This is working out really well*, I thought. After quite a few minutes on her back legs, I moved on to her toes, where she was dragging one foot. I felt that I needed to provide lots of energy to her hind-end area to help her move around better and improve her quality of life.

After an hour or more, the energy that I was provided waned, and I knew that I was done for now. I wished I could have kissed Hope on the head, but she was so peaceful that I didn't want to risk upsetting her. I would have to be satisfied that Rosanne would provide Hope with all the kisses I couldn't bestow on her.

It seems that kissing animals has always been my thing to express my love and joy to be with them. As a family, we visit a place called African Safari Wildlife Park in Port Clinton, Ohio, quite often, which is a drive-through zoo. We have taken most of my relatives and a ton of children through the years to this zoo to experience the up-close feel of the animals. Most of the animals they care for at the zoo roam free, and cars can drive through a designated area to visit with them, and you can feed them from your car. You are not allowed to leave your vehicle, but that doesn't stop me from hanging out of the windows and having the animals come close to the car to eat out of my hands and if I am lucky, receive a kiss.

I'll never forget the yelling my mother-in-law did when a giant, long-horned steer put his head through the open, front window of her brand-new car. I thought she was going to have a heart attack as I laughed like a hyena. The look on my husband's face the first time I called a buffalo to the car was priceless. He loves buffalo but had never been up close and personal with them. I felt he needed to have the experience, so naturally, I telepathically called them to me. In my life, I have had the pleasure of being kissed by zebras, giraffes, buffalo, elk, deer, and long-horned cattle, and they were the best kisses I ever had! Sorry to all the men in my life, but you can't compete even if you tried.

Hope had her good and bad days as was to be expected. On a routine basis, I would drive over to perform hands-on healing in addition to the distance healing that I sent nightly. Many of the healing techniques that I have in my proverbial toolbox require me to be actually present with my client. On this particular day, I was going over to introduce Hope to tuning forks. I love tuning forks; they feel funny in your hand as they are activated—soothing, almost like a vibrator. I learned about tuning forks in my HTA seminars.

I know you've probably heard that old adage that sound or music is said to soothe the savage beast. Did you know that many different sounds elicit reactions from animals and people alike? A gentle rain falling, waves crashing on the beach, or a gurgling brook are very calming, while a drum solo is very invigorating. You can almost feel the drums beating away inside your body. That's their vibration. Vibration comes in many forms. It can be loud, soft, or invigorating, or it can soothe you to sleep. I bet you never thought that it could also be used as a healing modality.

Physical bodies have many self-healing mechanisms. You cut yourself, and the wound will start to bleed, but your blood will eventually clot to stop the bleeding. That is your body self-healing. In music, what is known as an interval is the space between two notes. A pure fifth interval is mostly used for sound healing. With a tuning fork, the distance between tines is the pure fifth interval. A tuning fork is an acoustic, two-tined fork usually made of steel. It will resonate at a constant note when vibrated by striking it against an activator or surface. The pure musical tone and pitch depends on the length of the fork's tines. The frequency is measured in hertz. The hertz vibration is created when you hit the fork to an object or activator.

I use tuning forks in my holistic healing for both sound and vibrational therapy. The Om frequency (136.10 hertz), known as the earth's vibration, helps to enlist a deep relaxation within your pet and has many healing qualities. The Om frequency helps to facilitate the release of negativity in thoughts, emotions, and energy, causing healing. Earth vibrates at eight cycles (hertz) per second when it is calm—as do pets and people when the Om vibration is used. You can purchase Om tuning forks that are weighted to create the healing frequency. The three Om tuners I recommend are 90.73 hertz, that is, one and a half times lower frequency than Om; the Om frequency of 136.10 hertz, and 204.15 hertz, which is one and a half times higher than Om. The Om tuners that I've purchased are from Inner Sound and were developed by Arden and Jack Wilken.

To activate a tuning fork, hold the bottom shaft (skinny end) of the fork in your fingers and gently strike the flat, weighted side of the fork against an activator (rubber disk) or your arm/leg. You will see a slight movement in the tuning fork and will feel and hear the vibration this action creates. Put the fork up to your ear to experience what your pet will hear and feel. Make sure that you practice this activation several times to ensure that you are comfortable with the motion before using it on your pet.

In order to relax Hope for her tuning-fork healing session, I wanted her to become accustomed to the vibration and sound that the tuning fork created before I started to use it on her. To let her experience the sound and vibration, I simply activated the fork and held it about six inches from her nose. She could hear the soft vibration it made, which would help ease any fears she had and would ensure that she was used to the sound when I started to work with the fork around her head and body.

Vibrational therapy is accomplished by placing the fork on the body (muscles, bones, spine, or joints) to create balance in the energy system of a person or animal. I chose the first area of concern on Hope that I wanted to work on, which was her hips. I activated the tuning fork, and then I softly held the shaft of the fork on the right hip to elicit healing. I continued to hold the tuning fork there until the vibration stopped. I was able to feel when the vibration stopped because I was holding the fork by the shaft with my fingers.

I watched Hope for a reaction, but her eyes were soft and sort of dreamy looking; therefore, I assumed that it was okay to continue. She actually seemed to be enjoying the vibration on her body. This is normal, but I never know how an animal or person will react, so I proceed cautiously at first. I performed a set of three activations at her right hip. The first activation was done to open the energy system, the second cleared the energy, and the last created a balance within the energy system.

Vibrational therapy can help people and pets with numerous physical issues like arthritis, and it can help to facilitate healing of breaks, torn tendons, sore muscles, or any other injury. After I completed the series of three activations on her right hip, I moved on to her left hip and performed the same three activations. Hope was indeed happy with the session, as she presented me with a big yawn. Any kind of release, like yawning, sighing, or licking of the lips, is good to observe, as it means the animal is content with the healing technique. I continued on with my tuning-fork healing session, moving on to her paws—first the back right and then the back left—while activating the tuning fork three times each.

When I finished the bodywork on Hope using the vibrational therapy, I decided to use the tuning fork as sound therapy near Hope's ears without touching her body. I accomplished this by striking the fork to activate it and holding it next to her ear, about three to six inches away. I could have simply chosen to perform sound therapy on Hope's hips, legs, and paws instead of vibrational therapy, but I felt that she would benefit more from me actually placing the tine on her body. In addition, Hope didn't have any open wounds that I would hurt by touching her with the fork. Open sores or wounds are definitely a consideration when you choose to place a tuning fork on an animal's body to promote healing. I held the fork by her ear until it stopped vibrating completely, and then I performed the activation another two times. To help keep Hope in balance, I performed this sound therapy three times on each side of her head.

As a general rule, vibrational therapy will help to integrate other healing modalities that are offered, such as HTA, Reiki, TTouch, acupuncture, acupressure, and massage at a deeper level, and sound therapy will help to settle and ground your pet. Some uses or reasons to use tuning forks are:

- Creating relaxation, relieving stress
- Grounding and focusing, improving mental clarity and brain functions
- Stimulating the physiology of the body
- Speeding wound healing and fractures
- Helping with major illnesses
- Stabilizing for behavior modification
- Helping in animal hospice situations

Tuning forks are not expensive and can be purchased from many holistic wellness centers and through the Internet.

After our first tuning-fork healing session was completed, I showed Rosanne how the tuning forks worked. She was fascinated by the vibration and the sound that it made. I activated the Om fork and put it on Rosanne's knee so she could experience the sensation.

"No wonder the animals like this so much!" she exclaimed. "It is soothing and tranquil."

"I totally agree. I use them on myself all the time." I explained to Rosanne all the areas on Hope's body where she could use the tuning forks and then asked if she would like to keep them for a while to use on Hope on a regular basis.

"Oh my. Are you sure you want to leave them with me to use?" she inquired.

"No problem. Hope needs them more than I do, that's for sure. A routine tuning-fork session will be very beneficial for Hope's back legs and may help to strengthen them to enable her to walk better. I highly encourage you to do it as often as you can, as you cannot overdo this healing modality."

Rosanne was very grateful for the use of the tuning forks and the guidance. She was learning a great deal about holistic healing as she endeavored to make Hope comfortable.

Rosanne frequently sent me cards and little gifts to thank me for my support of her and Hope. Since we first found out Hope was terminal, I had decided that I would not charge for my time, so her tokens of thanks were very endearing to me and much appreciated. I kept all her cards and gifts. Many of them brought me to tears, as they were so heartfelt and loving. I actually don't think I deserved them, because although Hope was getting better at times, inevitably we all knew that we couldn't change what was to be. We could just attempt to keep her comfortable and happy with a good quality of life. I had never been through anything this intense with one of my clients before, and it was shaking me to my very soul. Sure, I had lost family members and pets in the past, but the emotional ups and downs of Hope's illness were profound. I kept telling myself that once it was all over, I would still be able to "talk" with her, and I comforted myself with that thought.

I doubted that fact would have been of much comfort to Rosanne, so I never mentioned it. She had enough on her plate just keeping Hope comfortable in her day-to-day routine. *It's funny*, I thought. *You work so hard to help someone and get so caught up in their care that you don't even look down the road to see where you are going with this. You simply just keep on giving.* Our stamina and determination in the face of horrific events is amazing. We are truly all made of pure love, just like our animal companions.

Lights, Camera, Action?

When Rosanne called me on March 3 to set up our next in-person healing session, I told her that I wanted to extend our healing with lights using a new technology I'd just purchased recently called the STS-2 healing system. This healing system is a two-part process. It has a scanner that allows me to physically scan an animal or human body externally to locate where any problems exist, and the lights allow me to localize the healing to a specific area.

When living tissue is damaged or injured, there is an immediate drop in the resistance to electrical impulses in that location. This means there is an increase in the ease with which the electrical impulses can move through the area. The scanner emits a very tiny electrical current called a microcurrent, which is like a nerve impulse in your body. The person or animal being treated cannot feel this current, just as the person administering the treatment also cannot, but it's used by the scanner to measure the resistance in the tissue it is touching at the time. If the resistance is low, the scanner will beep, telling me that there is a problem at that location on the client's body. I can detect a problem in the tissue when I touch it with the scanner probe; this is how I find an issue with muscles, joints, and tendons.

The scanner has the ability to locate acupuncture points. Active acupuncture points are points on the surface of the animal's or person's body that relate to other areas of the body that are having trouble. For example, there are over twelve hundred acupuncture points on a horse's body, but only those related to the area having the problem will be active. Lung, bladder, and intestine points are all examples of acupuncture points the scanner can locate. The great part of this process is that the scanner can indicate the point that needs work, and I can use light therapy on that point. Usually, areas with problems relate to an out-of-balance condition within the animal's body, and the treatment will help the overall condition of the animal.

The second part of the STS-2 system is the actual lights that work with a red light wavelength of 660 nanometers and infrared at 880 nanometers. I use the lights on the points where the scanner found a problem. The lights use red and infrared light to stimulate the injured area of the animal or person to heal faster and stronger than normal. Scientific studies along with thousands of clinical tests have shown that certain wavelengths of light (red and infrared) pulsed at specific frequencies can dramatically stimulate and accelerate the healing process.

Each of the power lights has twenty-four infrared and twenty-five red LEDs. Because the system allows me to program both the frequency and time exposure for the optimal effect, it can run for twenty to thirty seconds, and then we let nature take its course. The light therapy will stimulate immediately, but often the improvements will continue for forty-eight to seventy-two hours. I cannot burn the animal/person or cause any other problems.

Rosanne was all for this new technology, and we planned to meet the next Saturday for Hope's STS-2 healing. When Saturday arrived, I was packed up early, anxiously awaiting our designated time to meet so that I could begin the healing session.

I decided that it would be a benefit to all of us to ensure that Hope was accepting of this healing contraption, as it was in a large case; therefore, I brought lavender essential oil to use on her. Lavender essential oil is very calming for people and animals, which is why many lavender pillows are sold to lull people to sleep.

After our initial greeting of hugs and kisses, we sat down to get to work. I explained to Rosanne, "I am going to chill Hope out a bit by letting her smell or lick, whichever she prefers, some lavender essential oil. It works to help calm and relax both people and pets. All I have to do is offer it to her in my hand. Don't be alarmed if she licks it, as it is perfectly safe for her to ingest it." I shook two or three drops of the lavender essential oil onto the palm of my hand, placed my hands together, and then moved them clockwise for several rotations. "I am doing this to activate the oil. Now I will open my hands and offer it to Hope." Hope took a tentative sniff and proceeded to lick my hand. "Excellent!" I exclaimed. "I am happy she took the oil in both through her nose and by ingestion. Let's just sit and minute and let that work on her, and by the way, I'll leave the bottle with you, and you can use it whenever you wish, even on yourself!"

We chatted for a few minutes, and then I started to open up the STS-2 system to begin my work. Since Rosanne and I spoke about the healing system and how it worked on the phone, we had decided that it would be best for Hope to just begin to heal the areas we knew had problems without doing a full body scan on her. We both felt that the high-pitched sound that the system emitted when it found an issue would make Hope uptight and fearful. We didn't want to stress her out any more than necessary with all our healing equipment.

I pulled all the healing paddles in and set the appropriate level of power on the machine. I then placed the two paddles gently on Hope's hip area first and held them there for thirty seconds. Then I moved the paddles to the next location on Hope's body, performing the same movements over and over until I covered the entire back portion of her body. Hope gave me some weird looks but then seemed to relax and let me do my thing.

I taught Rosanne how to work the paddles and the healing system. Then I put it away in its protective case, and I pulled out the next healing tool from the STS-2 system. I explained to Rosanne, "This is a healing pad, which looked similar to a normal heating pad but longer in length. The pad, which has funny tiny bulbs attached to it, was originally designed to cover a horse's back for healing purposes and consists of an infrared and red lights. The pad can be used several times a day on specific areas of an animal's body. This type of pad is very helpful with bone, tendon, or muscle issues. You don't need any type of training to use it, as it almost works like a heating pad, without the heat, and it turns itself off after thirty minutes of use." I told Rosanne that I felt it would work wonderfully for Hope. I showed her how to plug the cords into the setting box and how to schedule the healing level.

It was so simple that I knew she would love to use it. Hope could just lie next to her on the floor or on the couch, if she could get up, and they could watch TV together with the pad on Hope. Since Hope was not moving around a lot anymore, it would work perfectly for her. I worked with the healing light a total of forty-five minutes, which in hindsight was probably too much. I left the STS-2 healing system and light pad with Rosanne for future use when needed.

Hope had an adverse reaction to the healing-light session. Maybe it was too intense for her body, but after I left, her legs gave out, and she seemed like she was in a lot of pain and was passing gas. I believe this was her body's way of eliminating toxins, but we didn't want Hope in any pain. Before her therapy, her stool was very long, Tootsie Roll shaped, and soft and whitish in color. Right after I left the healing session, she eliminated three Tootsie Roll–shaped stools, soft and normal color; however, two hours later, her legs gave out, and she was in a lot of pain and was passing gas again. Rosanne called me to help her. (It reminded me of Thanksgiving all over again.) Rosanne mentioned that Hope was not moving much these days unless she was out of her sight or no one else was sitting with her.

Rosanne called me around 2:00 p.m., and I immediately went to work on Hope from a distance. I used my surrogate stuffed animal and worked for approximately thirty minutes, moving the energy through her system and hopefully out. It wasn't until 9:30 p.m. that evening that Hope was able to get up and go outside to eliminate on her own, seemingly without any pain.

I had left Rosanne my tuning fork, and she applied twenty-five minutes of vibrational therapy on Hope's back legs. Rosanne observed and documented that Hope did nothing but deposit golden mush all day. Her right hind leg was extremely swollen. Rosanne sat with her and iced it as she watched a movie. Hope showed no interest in eating that day; therefore, Rosanne cooked a few of Hope's favorites just to get her to eat something. She managed to tempt her to eat scrambled eggs, dried duck hearts, and ground beef. *Yum!* Mom sure knows how to cook.

The next day was the turning point with Hope's bathroom situation. Every time Hope tried to eliminate, she would make a sound like it was hurting her. She tried four times to poop, and she deposited nothing but mush. Rosanne provided Hope with another twenty minutes with the tuning fork vibrational therapy, because she really felt this healing modality was helping Hope to get up and down on her own power. She ate real salmon with her hard food for breakfast and cooked chicken with her hard food for dinner. Cottage cheese was her cold snack during the day. Another good day of eating!

On March 6, Hope slept by the Christmas tree all night. She woke up licking her right hind leg and had inadvertently removed some hair, creating a hot spot. She was shivering. She got up to pee; however, her back right leg was badly swollen and not working at all, which caused her to drag it. Rosanne immediately iced the inside of her right hind leg and on top of her hip three times throughout the day. The family brought her water to her so that she wouldn't get up unnecessarily, as they did not want her to become dehydrated. This was one of the last days she pooped, and when she did, she groaned to squeeze out whatever was left after walking around.

Coloring, Anyone?

Hope had her next appointment with Dr. P. on March 6, but she couldn't make it, because Rosanne wasn't able to lift her into the car, and Hope herself could only walk a tiny distance without her help. I was at work, so I was useless to them in that situation. I suggested that we try something else since Hope couldn't go.

On March 7, Rosanne and I arranged to try another holistic method of healing for our next hands-on session. She, as always, was all for it! Hope had been in a funk lately and did not seem to be as happy as she could have been. I felt that attempting to use color healing would perk her up a bit since it was winter and because she wasn't well enough to spend time outside. Hope loved the snow, so it broke Rosanne's heart that she didn't seem to enjoy it anymore.

Rosanne was open to all my "teachable moments," wanting to learn all she could about holistically healing. She had completed her level-one Reiki class and was using it daily on Hope, but I think she felt she wasn't good enough and wanted to do everything she could for Hope. I completely understood, as there is nothing like the feeling you get when you know you are helping someone feel better. It is like God is working through you, and the experience is remarkable.

I explained to Rosanne that every living being has an energy system, and keeping that energy system functioning effectively or restoring balance is achievable by using color. Using color therapies is simply preventative care. Color therapy has been known to strengthen, cleanse, invigorate, and balance, and it may regulate metabolic processes, positively influencing bodily functions and moods. When I use color to heal, I am actively engaging in my own health maintenance and that of the animal I am working on. Color therapy is not practicing medicine. We are simply using knowledge to help others holistically feel better.

I decided to tease Rosanne a little bit to get her to understand how color works. "So, Rosanne, are you in the pink today? Do you feel blue? Seeing the world through rose-colored glasses again? Are you green with envy at the neighbor's new car? I bet all these phrases sound familiar to you. You've heard them a hundred times in your life. We've all relied on color to make us feel better, to describe where we are emotionally, or to provide a pick-me-up. Doesn't seeing a rainbow bring a smile to your face and peace into your heart? It does for me! All those beautiful colors shining in the sky are magical," I explained.

"Color, simply put, is a concentration of light frequency. To see color, you have to have light. When light shines on an object, some colors bounce off the object, and others are absorbed by it. All light rays contain color, and our world is full of light. The sun's rays contain all the colors of the rainbow mixed together. Light is made of electromagnetic waves. These waves spread out from any light source, such as the sun. Light waves travel at tremendous speed (186,000 miles, or 300,000 kilometers per second). Different colors have different wavelengths. Visible light is made of seven wavelength groups. These are the colors you see in a rainbow: red, orange, yellow, green, blue, indigo, and violet. The longest wavelength of light that humans can see is red, with the shortest being violet. Ultraviolet has an even shorter wavelength, but humans cannot see it. Some birds and bees can see ultraviolet light. Infrared has a longer wavelength than red light, and humans cannot see this light but can feel the heat infrared generates.

"Color falls into three categories: the primary colors, which are red, blue, and yellow. The secondary colors, orange, green and violet, are made from mixing primary colors together. When you mix primary and secondary colors, you create tertiary colors, which are red violet, blue violet, yellow orange, red orange, yellow green, and blue green. Color models for light use red, green and blue as primary colors, with red and green making yellow light.

"You've probably heard that some colors are considered 'warm' like red, while other colors are considered 'cool' like blue. It is correct to assume that the more red a color has in it, the warmer the color will be; likewise, the more blue a color has in it, the cooler it will be. This information is very useful when choosing a color to heal with.

"Now that I've told you how we see color and what it actually is, let's talk about how I'm going to apply color to facilitate healing with Hope. As you've learned through all the healings that I have performed on your doggie, the human and animal bodies are energy systems. All energy follows thought; therefore, as you think about a specific color, that color will be transmitted to your hands. You can then use your hands to help various physical or emotional issues through your touch on problem areas. Remember, it's all about your intention! To use the hand technique to send color, take a few breaths in through your nose and out your mouth to establish a relaxed breathing rhythm. Place your hands over Hope approximately three to six inches off her body. Envision pure white energy coming in through the top of your head and down through your arms to your hands. Continue this process for a few minutes, and then proceed to place your hands on or by the problem area you are healing, and bring the appropriate color for that issue into your mind. Send that color down your arms and out your hands for approximately five minutes. Now that I've explained it, let's have you try it."

Rosanne proceeded to do as I instructed while I watched over her. She was doing a great job, and I was impressed with her concentration and willingness to learn. *Okay*, I thought, *let's shake things up a bit!* I wanted to teach Rosanne another way to bring color to her life.

I told her, "An additional way to heal using color is to perform color breathing. In order to begin the process for healing yourself, sit in a comfortable place with your spine straight. Put the tip of your tongue against the roof of your mouth just behind your front teeth. Inhale slowly through your nostrils for a count of six. Hold that breath for a slow count of approximately twelve, and then slowly exhale through your mouth for another slow count of six if you can." I had her try this and told her to keep doing the breathing technique until she had a slow rhythm.

"Now here is the next trick," I said. "Once your breathing has been established, try to see and feel the air that you are breathing coming in as a specific color, using your imagination and intention. Let this color fill your entire body. Think that this color is correcting any issues that you have, either emotional or physical. If you are not sure of the color to use, you can just use white light or all the colors of the rainbow. Keep breathing the color you have chosen for approximately five minutes," I coached. She was doing fabulous and was not hyperventilating, so I determined that she was ready to try this new technique on Hope.

"To heal Hope, just transmit the color healing by breathing on her using a piece of cloth of the appropriate color where she requires healing. I brought blue, which should help with the cancer. Lay the cloth where the cancer is located in her body." I handed the swatch of fabric to Rosanne, and she almost reverently placed the cloth on Hope. I continued with my instruction by encouraging her to establish her rhythmic breathing, envisioning the color she wanted. "Exhale and place your mouth very close to the blue cloth, and then breathe onto it. Set your intention that your breath will be absorbed into her body, healing it. Keep doing this process for several minutes until you feel that healing has begun.

"Breathing different colors will help with specific health issues. The key is how to know what color to use."

I've provided a list in the additional resource section of this book to help the reader determine the appropriate color to choose for your healing experience. Remember, if you do not know what the emotional or physical problem is, just send white or all the colors of the rainbow.

"So, Rosanne, what have you learned?" I inquired.

Rosanne perked up and said, "Intention and thought is the key!"

"You are a quick study. I'll make a healer out of you yet." I laughed. "Don't forget to be creative. You don't have to follow any of the methods I just taught you. Find a method you like. If you would like, you can use colored stones, tissue paper, or colored cellophane rubber-banded on a small flashlight—the sky is the limit!

"In fact, I have another tool to show you—my Lumalight. The Lumalight looks like sophisticated small flash light and it was developed by Julianne Bien of Spectrahue Color Hamonics. She is a wonderful person and teacher. The Lumalight is a revolutionary color and geometry light set which has been enhanced with Spectrahue Vibration Technology for purity in color harmonic vibrations."

"As a healer of both people and pets, I have one full box of different colors, but you can purchase a full set, which is two boxes of a variety of colors plus geometric metal symbols to use within the light set. I never felt I needed the full set, because my main focus is animal communications, but this healing modality sure can help both people and animals. The color harmonics healing technique I use promotes wellness in your pet. The Lumalight uses color therapy as an energy healing-based modality. The Lumalight tool is used by many holistic energy workers and in home practice as a stand-alone wellness modality or in conjunction with other types of energy healing. Animals are similar to humans in that they exhibit a meridian system. Our animal's meridian system has energy channels for the body, activated by light."

Defeated

Because of Hope's issues with eating, she was now fed Hill's Critical Care soft food mixed with cooked chicken. On March 7, she did not get up at all until 11:40 a.m. to pee, which was very unusual. She was only able to rise after having fifteen minutes of the STS-2 healing lights. I had left the system with Rosanne for her use during the time I was not available to be with them.

As the day went on, Hope began to pee where she lay. Rosanne told me she put big-girl pants on Hope with feminine hygiene pads inside to help absorb the moisture. It had come to Hope now needing assistance to get up and walk around outside. After dinner, her attempt to poop was accomplished, but it had no substance at all. In fact, she had to have the underside of her body cleansed outside on the back porch before entering the house to cuddle on the floor with her family.

Days earlier, Rosanne arranged for an assistant from Dr. P.'s office to come to her home to provide more holistic energy healing for Hope since she could no longer transport her to the vet's office.

It obviously helped, because Hope hadn't eaten breakfast that morning but thoroughly enjoyed her dinner of cooked turkey with yogurt. She again pooped once in the evening as mushy and messy as the night before. Another wipe down was needed. Rosanne told me it was like having a large child to clean up after.

The next day, Hope was unable to eliminate her bowels altogether and was not able to move around freely. It seemed as if she couldn't walk at all, which was a first. Hope's back right leg was so swollen that she needed the family's help to move her. She ate very little. Rosanne's son carried her bed back and forth from the bedroom to the back room for her to be with them. She would attempt to get up and move but only for a brief moment.

The family carried on with assisting Hope to go outside with a towel strapped under her. They used the towel to hold up her body weight while she walked and peed outside. She was not having a bowel movement, and getting her to eat was becoming a challenge.

Wouldn't you know, the next day the weather was absolutely beautiful? The family took Hope outside to bask in the sun several times. Rosanne took a picture of Hope in the grass, and she looked like a puppy again. Unfortunately, they had to start to feed Hope by hand just to get her to eat something throughout the day. It wasn't only the family who were outside that day. The four-month-old Christmas tree had to be thrown out, as it was losing its needles by the bucketful. They instinctively knew they wouldn't have long with Hope now, as the Christmas tree seemed to be in sync with Hope's condition, and it symbolized the hopefulness they carried in their heart.

Rosanne was in constant contact with me regarding Hope's downward spiral, and I was healing and talking to Hope almost nonstop even while I was at work for the last week or more. I asked Hope, "Do you feel your time with the family is up? Do you want assistance out of your body?" I explained to Hope what I meant by assistance, telling her about the shot and how she would simply go to sleep and then become spirit to watch over the family. I did not tell Rosanne what I was talking about with Hope. I needed to know for myself what Hope was thinking in order to be prepared to console Rosanne through the hardest decision she would ever make. I knew it was just around the corner; I felt it in the core of my being. We'd worked so hard to give Hope a good quality of life, but I felt it was futile to try any longer, as I knew she was now suffering more than we anticipated. I didn't want to fail Hope in her last moment of need. I prayed for clarity and a head free of my own agenda.

She replied to me, "Yes, I think it may be necessary. I remember what it is like to be out of my body (in spirit). I am not worried. I love my family so much. They did everything they could for me, and I feel guilty that I have caused so much heartache and trouble to them."

I told her, "Do not worry about that. They cared for you because you are a member of their family, the love of their lives. You have given so much to them already. They only care about your comfort and well-being. Whatever you decide will be okay with them. They will accept your decision."

She replied, "I do not want to leave them, but my body is giving out. I can see that now. I would like assistance if that is possible. Please tell them how grateful I am for all the love and care they provided to me. I was supposed to take care of them! I will be back to do just that. I love them and will be with them always. Please tell them!"

"I will, Hope. You are very brave, and I admire your will and determination through your illness. It has been an honor to get to know you and help you in any way I could. Contact me when you become spirit, as I can talk to you there also. Your words will comfort your family a great deal. They will want to know that you are all right. I can also assist you when you wish to return, so just call on me whenever you need me. If I am not listening, as I get so caught up in my day-to-day life, do something to get Mom's attention. I know she will call me to understand what she saw. I will then know that you want to talk, and I will connect with you. Be free, my friend."

Rosanne went to work the following day while her son Mackenzie stayed home with Hope. He could only get her outside twice, and he pretty much carried her the whole way. She called her local vet's office and asked if she could bring Hope in for an enema because she had not eliminated for almost three days. Always hopeful she was. The vet's office gave Hope a 5:30 p.m. appointment. Rosanne contacted me to let me know of her call to her vet and the scheduled time she was given to have Hope at their office. I knew I had to express to her my feelings and what Hope had told me. That was my job as an animal communicator—to tell their owners their thoughts and wishes. This was not going to be easy for Rosanne to hear or for me to say, but I could not fail Hope when she needed me the most.

I began my conversation with Rosanne with the fact that I talked to Hope about how she was feeling. I explained that she knew her body was giving out and that she wanted assistance out of her body. I knew Rosanne didn't want to hear that message. I comforted her with the fact that we had all worked extremely hard with all the love we had in our hearts to ensure that Hope was comfortable and not in any pain, and now the time had come where we could do no more for her. Hope understood that she couldn't get better and didn't want the family fussing over her. She was ready to leave. I'm not sure what Rosanne was thinking as she listened quietly. We were both crying softly as I tried to express Hope's wishes. Rosanne had to leave for the vet appointment, and I wasn't sure what the outcome was going to be. I knew she'd heard what I'd told her, but I didn't know if she'd accepted it and would be able to act upon it. I prayed for us all but especially for strength and support from all the healing angels, Rosanne's guides, Jesus, Saint Francis, God, and the Holy Spirit (yes, I'm Catholic). I knew the family was going to need all the support they could get.

Rosanne arrived home from work, ran into the house, and dropped to the floor to hug and kiss her beautiful baby girl. She had a permanent spot in the back room on Murray's dog bed, where she had a beautiful view looking out the sliding glass doors at her backyard. Hope by now was not able to move unless they helped her. Her leg was so swollen that she could not use it to lift herself. Mackenzie had stayed home with her all day, sitting with her on the floor, watching TV together. Once Rosanne's husband, Michael, came home, the boys carried Hope out to the car with Hope on top of the dog bed. Rosanne told me that Hope looked like she was on a magic carpet ride. With Mackenzie sitting next to her, Hope perked up and lifted her body, leaning onto the backseat so that she could watch out the window. She looked so peaceful.

Once they arrived at the vet office, the boys carried Hope into the waiting room on her bed. They were taken right in into an exam room. They kept Hope on her bed, for she was very comfortable and again was not able to lift herself without assistance. The vet assistant greeted them and Hope and then quietly asked if they were considering euthanizing Hope that day. Rosanne said, "No, I was hoping that she could receive an enema to help her poop." The assistant left the room only to return with one of the vets that usually took care of Hope at her physicals. They, of course, knew all what was going on with Hope but had not seen her for two months because she was working with Dr. P.

The vet asked what was going on, and Rosanne told her about Hope's inability to defecate and that it had been three days since she had last gone to the bathroom. They were wondering if the vet could give Hope an enema to help the blockage. The vet began to lecture Rosanne as she placed a rubber glove on her hand to give Hope a rectal exam. Her tone of voice became firm and loud, yelling at her that Hope was in pain and couldn't she see that, and that the cancer was taking a toll on Hope. Rosanne, being the ever-vigilant mother hen, lashed back at her, stating that Hope was not in pain, but she did not go any further with her comment, because she already knew that this particular doctor did not believe in Reiki or holistic medicine.

The vet asked if Hope was on any pain medicines (that which they would have prescribed, not what Hope had been receiving from Dr. P.), and Rosanne told them no, which really seemed to set her on fire. In the meantime, she was slightly surprised to see the results of the rectal exam. Hope's feces were soft, and her anal area was moist with muscle contractions. Rosanne thought this would stop the well-intentioned vet from lashing out because she thought the family was making Hope suffer.

The vet said she could not give Hope an enema, for they would have to sedate her, and they were not sure what they would encounter once they started. What seemed like forever was a thirty-minute bashing of how, when, and why the vet thought it best to euthanize Hope. Rosanne was the only one speaking on behalf of Hope in that office. Her husband and son stayed quiet. The doctor and assistant dismissed themselves, giving the family a few minutes to think things over. Through all this, Hope never moved. She was tightly pressed against Rosanne's stomach with Rosanne's arm wrapped around her.

Once the doctor left the room, Rosanne latched on to Hope around the neck and told her that Mommy was sorry. She did not know what to do. She asked her husband, and he promptly replied that it was her decision to make. Rosanne squatted in front of Hope and stared into her eyes, holding her face softly in her hands. She did not want Hope to see her cry, but there was no other expression she could muster. Rosanne then stood up, wrapped her arms around Hope, and quietly fought with the thoughts in her head. She had never had to make this decision before. All of her other pets had passed away at home. She knew if they left with her, it would be even harder for her to bring Hope back, knowing what would be awaiting for Hope when they returned. She decided to do what she had to do. All of a sudden, her insides seemed to be at peace, as if there were no worries. She lovingly kissed Hope and then turned to Mackenzie and asked him to call his brother.

Once they had Mitch on the phone, Rosanne quietly explained the situation and that they were going to release the cancer from her body. They were going to set her free. He wanted to say good-bye to Hope, so Rosanne held the phone up to Hope's ears as Mitch told her how much he loved her and that she would always be with him in his heart forever. He said more, but Rosanne blocked out hearing any other words by that point. Hope had shown she was done talking by lifting her head toward Rosanne. Rosanne said good-bye to Mitch and told him how sorry she was.

Rosanne opened the exam room door a crack to wave the assistant into the room. She told her they would be saying their good-byes and that they were ready. The doctor came into the room minutes later, set up her table, and then explained what they were going to do and what would happen. She would not let Rosanne hold Hope during the procedure, for it was against their policy. Again, Rosanne squatted down in front of Hope and held her head gently for the last time. They stared into each other's eyes as she whispered to her, "Always remember, you are so beautiful, so brave, and so strong, and Mommy loves you very much. Please don't ever forget that." Rosanne lovingly kissed her on her nose, and Hope gently kissed her back.

The assistant shaved a small portion of hair from Hope's arm as the family stepped away. The doctor explained what would happen next, but Rosanne could not watch. She hid behind her husband, crying. She told me that all she could remember was the doctor telling them that Hope was gone. She thought to herself, *A life, gone that quickly.* Only seconds for her best friend to be set free. She made her way over to Hope, standing by her head and neck. She hugged her tightly telling her how sorry she was that she couldn't save her, that she hoped she was running and enjoying life as she had before.

The assistant came back into the room and made a paw-print keepsake for the family to take home. They requested to have their beloved family pet cremated. Hope transitioned into spirit at 6:15 p.m. on Monday, March 12, 2012. It was a very dark day for the family.

After arriving home, Rosanne stepped outside to call me. She said she was so glad I answered the phone.

The dreaded phone call came as I was cooking dinner for my family. I always knew it would come, but I was caught off guard nevertheless. Rosanne was on the phone sobbing, which I knew was not a good thing, and all she said was, "She's gone."

I screamed, "What!" and immediately broke into tears. We were connected together through our crying, no one talking, just sobbing, sometimes quietly and sometimes hysterically. My husband immediately came over to see what the problem was, and I mouthed to him that Hope was gone. He put his arms around me and rocked me back and forth as I cried with the phone cradled to my ear. Even our husky got in on the act. It seemed like time stood still. I am not really sure how long we stayed on the phone together crying. I tried to pull myself together for Rosanne's sake. I tried to provide words of encouragement, but I am sure they sounded hollow. Nothing could fix this. I remember her telling me that Hope helped her make the decision. She said that a sense of peace came over her while she struggled with the decision, and she knew that was her answer.

Rosanne asked me to connect with Hope, to see if she was okay. I said, "Please be aware that it is not uncommon that for a period of time I cannot connect with a spirit, especially if they have just passed."

I immediately tried to contact Hope, and I smiled gratefully when I heard her tell me, "Look, look, I am running." Rosanne told me that she remembered smiling with tears pouring down her face when she heard that, as she looked up to the sky trying to imagine her beautiful girl running free at last. I told her what I was experiencing, which was Hope in a beautiful field being greeted by Rosanne's dear neighbor Dorothea, who then showed Hope around her flower garden.

Rosanne and I talked for about an hour, and she asked me to keep in touch with Hope. After a while, we both decided to disconnect, as I knew she needed to be comforted by her family as well as to provide it to her boys. At least they had each other and, of course, the other pets in the household. I didn't try to contact Hope, as I knew she was in the midst of her transition, and I didn't want to keep pulling her spirit back down to earth for selfish reasons. Her spirit must go to the light; besides, I knew she would be just fine in heaven. Coming from a Catholic upbringing, I believe that we all are destined for heaven. I have spoken with many people and pets that have passed into spirit, and they always tell me about who met them and what it is like to be in spirit. I'll never forget my dad's words to me the first time he came through to me in spirit.

He said, "It's just like you said, Diane, I am right here. Tell your sister I am right here. I can practically touch you. It's like a film is in the way, but I can see everything."

I laughed and told him, "I know, Daddy, and I will definitely tell Debbie." He had come roaring into my face with a cigar in his mouth. I found that very odd, because he had given up cigars more than ten years earlier when my mom passed away. I asked him, "Daddy, what are you doing with that cigar in your mouth?"

He laughed and quickly replied, "Your mother wanted to see it."

I thought about that for an instant and then smiled broadly with a grin that didn't leave my face for quite a while as I realized what he had said to me. He was with my mom! They were together. My sister and I couldn't have asked for anything better. I could not wait to tell her! My mom had never known my dad to not have a cigar hanging out of his mouth, so it made perfect sense that she wanted to see him with it again.

Gone for Now but Not Forever

Rosanne called me over to pick up some of Hope's toys and things that she thought the shelter where I volunteer would like to use. When I was in her kitchen talking to both her and Mitch, her son, I found that Hope wanted to interrupt our conversation. I, naturally, let her.

Hope wanted to let everyone know that she was fine and able to walk and run really well again. She stated that she knew that would be very important for Mom to know. Rosanne was smiling when I provided that information to her. We only wanted Hope's happiness; after all, that was really what the last six months was about.

"Tell them I am fine. I will come back. Mitch will be the one to find me. He will find me online, and they will recognize me by my ears. They will be the same." Hope had very large ears that stood straight up, larger than most shepherd mixes. It had been her dominant feature.

"It won't be for a while yet, but I will contact you when I am ready and obtain permission," she continued to say.

I relayed the information to mom and son and told them that it was not unusual to have to arrange to come back. Everything would need to be aligned with the universe ahead of time.

Rosanne told me that she knew and apologized for being a pest for the first month after Hope passed, wanting to talk with Hope and asking when she could come back home. Once Hope said that she would love to come back, that was all Rosanne ever thought of. She told me that her heart was heavy and that she couldn't forgive herself for how Hope's life ended.

I continued to counsel Rosanne that Hope had to go through a transition and that if the time was right, based on what was going on with Rosanne, maybe she would be granted reincarnation. The biggest issue would be if Hope desired to come back, and obviously she did.

Rosanne would call me and ask, "Why can't I feel or notice Hope visiting me? I have not felt her presence or seen her in my dreams!"

I responded, "You are in an emotional place right now. Hope felt it was best not to visit so soon. Hope has been in the backyard protecting it. She has been there for a while now just hanging out."

Once Rosanne heard that, she took one of Hope's bones and placed it outside for her to have. She never moved it from the spot where she placed it.

On March 19, 2012, Rosanne received a letter from the American Holistic Veterinary Medical Association advising her that Dr. P. had made a donation to their foundation in memory of Hope. The donation was to help the association with their efforts to advance holistic veterinary medicine so it would be furthered for humane and ethical research. You go, Dr. P.!

One month after Hope's passing, Rosanne wrote me a thank you-note in memory of Hope. In the note, she wrote, "You were the one who gave me hope. You were the one who told me the truth. You dropped everything you were doing several times to help Hope in her weakest moments. You searched for miracles to save my baby girl. You brought Hope and me even closer by the journey we took together. You provided peace and dignity for my little girl. You were and still are our earth angel!" I will cherish that letter forever. They were the nicest, kindest words anyone has ever said to me. I smiled sadly just thinking about all we had endured and accomplished with Hope, yet it didn't seem like it was enough.

Throughout out the spring and summer, both Rosanne and I thought of Hope often. I talked to her many times; however, as anxious as Rosanne was to have her back, Hope was not ready. Sometime midsummer 2012, while I was talking with Hope, I found out that she was ready to come back home. I explained to Rosanne that Hope had to confer with her spirit guides and angels to complete her process in heaven. I knew that Rosanne already had a name for the new puppy cemented in her mind. It would be *Faith*, because she had *Hope* (literally), and now she was putting all her faith in the reincarnation process. Rosanne had all along thought that she would find Hope in a shelter. However, on Hope's birthday in September, out of the blue, Hope came to me and told me that she had put all the pieces in place and had worked with her guides and angels to come back into physical form. She was ready. Talk about your synchronicities! I was ecstatic to say the least. Wait until Rosanne heard this! She would be so happy. Rosanne was in her driveway, stretching before a run, when I placed the call she had been waiting for. I must have had a very excitable tone in my voice, but I did not start our conversation with why I was calling. I informed her that I was the messenger from Hope and that she received approval to come home. As I predicted, Rosanne went nuts with enthusiasm, to the point where I had to calm her down.

"She's not coming yet," I counseled. "She just arranged everything to enable her to physically come back. Now all the pieces have to fall together, and then she will tell me when she's ready." Rosanne was full of questions, and her excitement knew no bounds. I laughed and said, "Calm down. She'll be here soon enough."

Rosanne shared with me months later how she recalled that evening's phone call. She told me that her emotions were over the moon with excitement and that she remembered telling me that it was Hope's birthday and that Hope just received a wonderful present, that we all received a present on her birthday. Hope's birthday was not really known for sure, but her foster mom had information from the animal shelter's vet that Hope was twelve weeks old on December 3. Having this information, it was easy to calculate approximately when Hope was really born. Rosanne decided that since the calculation put Hope's birthday at the beginning of September, she would bestow her grandmother's birthday to Hope as her birthday, September 4. Rosanne mentioned she was dancing in the dark with so much excitement that after we hung up, she ran her best time for two miles in over thirty years. Her adrenaline was soaring, and she could recall telling herself that she needed to become a stronger runner so she and Hope could run together again.

"But how will we know her? How will we find her? Where should we look?" the questions kept tumbling out of Rosanne's mouth.

"Slow down and breathe," I told her. "We'll figure it all out together with Hope's help. I'll contact her again in a few weeks and see what progress she has made and if she can tell me anything that will help our search." I could tell that I let the wind out of Rosanne's sails, but she had to know that the miracle that she had been waiting for would still require some time yet.

"Promise you'll tell me everything the minute you hear from her, okay?"

Laughing at her enthusiasm, I replied, "I most certainly will. You will be the first to know!"

While Hope was not physically with Rosanne, she was still behind the scenes in the family's life, arranging miracles herself. During a very nasty rainstorm that hit Ohio, Rosanne's husband saw a little black dog hiding under a picnic table in the Metroparks. He pulled over and playfully called the dog to him. The puppy ran to Michael and excitedly smothered him with kisses. He immediately called Rosanne, asking what to do with the pup, to which she replied, "Bring him home. I will call the shelter and police departments around to see if someone has posted a lost dog that fits his description."

Rosanne called me two days later to inquire if this puppy was Hope. After all, the dog was black, a puppy, and male, and he made himself right at home in their household. I contacted my spirit guides who told me, no, this was not Hope; however, Hope had helped orchestrate her husband finding this pup. Hope talked with the scared puppy, telling him that a nice man would be driving by soon and would stop for him. She told the puppy that he should not be afraid. The nice man would take care of him and keep him safe. The little pup now resides two doors down from them, and his new family named him Wilson. Wilson, the little pup, was immediately accepted by Rosanne's dog Murray and her cats, and he lived with Rosanne's family for a month before he went to their neighbors. They periodically take care of Wilson when his family travels, and he is a great playmate with Rosanne's dogs.

True to my word, I attempted to contact Hope in October to find out any information that she could supply to me that would assist our search for her. I cleared my mind and called for Hope, but she didn't answer. This was very unusual for me. I grounded myself, took a crystal that I used to assist in my telepathy with animals, and called for her again.

"Hope, Hope, where are you?" I waited and listened, but no one came through. I called in my spirit guides and Saint Francis to assist me in my communication. "Hope, are you there?" I said in a voice that was slightly panicky.

All of a sudden, another voice popped into my head and said, "She cannot talk right now, Diane, as she is in the womb. What is it that you require?"

I was startled by the news, and it took me a minute to recover my thoughts before I replied, "Who am I speaking with?"

"I am Hope's angel. You can contact me if you need her, but she is unable to communicate with you at this point. You will not be able to contact her directly until she is born."

This was a new experience for me, as I had never attempted to talk to an animal in utero before. "Thank you for letting me know. Please contact me when she is born."

"I most certainly will notify you, Diane."

I sat in my meditation room with my mind whirling. This important information that I never knew, and I had to explain it to Rosanne. She was not going to believe this. I called Rosanne immediately to give her my news. She was astounded, to say the least. Now we just had to wait.

Have you ever had a baby? If so, do you remember how excruciating the wait for him or her was? Well, that's where Rosanne and I were. I was going through uncharted territory as far as my animal communication business was concerned, and I couldn't wait to see where it would lead me. I had never coached an animal through reincarnation before, but here I was working it like a pro. I thank all my guides for their help, as I am sure I could never have done it without them. Rosanne and I began calculating when Hope might be born, based on the gestation period of dogs. We both knew nothing about this off the top of our heads, so Google searches were in order. We calculated that she would definitely be an early Christmas present. How appropriate was that in the scheme of things! We had previously worked so hard to have her with us through Christmas, and now she would be back again. Of course, I told Rosanne not to get too excited, because puppies could not be sold until they were at least six to eight weeks old, so we knew we had time to wait.

In the meantime, Rosanne and I were continuing on with our dull lives, working and taking care of our families as if nothing was happening. I was preparing my department to close up and move to a work-at-home scenario. It was a very busy time. On my last business trip, before I was to retire (early, mind you; I am not that old), almost a week after Thanksgiving, the long-awaited message came. I was on a plane, on my way to Jacksonville, Florida, and I just closed my eyes to rest them from reading when I heard a voice in my head say, "Hope is being born." My eyes popped open, and I looked around me to see who'd said it. It was so loud and clear it had to have come from someone close to me. No luck. Everyone was busy with their laptops, reading, or sleeping, and no one seemed to have spoken to me. I closed my eyes with a big grin on my face, cleared my mind, and said, "What did you say?"

A kind, gentle voice came through and said, "Hope is being born right now."

Still smiling, I replied, "Thank you so much for letting me know." I could not wait to get off the plane and get through with this business trip. Rosanne was going to flip out!

On Tuesday, December 4, 2012, at 8:08 p.m., I called Rosanne with the message she was waiting for. "Hi, Rosanne; it's Diane. Guess what I'm calling about? Someone's had a miracle! Actually, it happened last week when I was in Jacksonville, Florida, and I didn't have any free time to call. The surprise you've been waiting for happened on Wednesday—I think that was the twenty-eighth or twenty-ninth, I'm not sure. We'll count now six to eight weeks, and then we will have to start looking."

When Rosanne and I were finally able to hook up on the phone, she immediately started worrying about how she would find her and what type of dog we should be looking for. I, on the other hand, having full faith in the universe, said, "Don't worry! We will find her. The universe will lead us to her. I know this is a huge leap of faith, but I have confidence that she will come to you. Just sit back and let me handle the details." In my own mind and heart, I prayed to my guides, God, and Saint Francis to keep Hope healthy and to let us find her quickly before Rosanne went crazy!

I placed my thoughts of Hope on the back burner as I readied my household for the Christmas holiday season. With all the preparation that went into the holidays and closing down the department I worked in, I was extremely busy. Rosanne, on the other hand, was hard at work. She told me that after my phone call, she'd thought, *Six to eight weeks, my ass!* She immediately started looking on the Internet. She didn't know what she was looking for, but her first thought was a rescue.

Poor Mitch! Rosanne drove him nuts all through December. They were checking everything, everywhere, from southern Ohio to western Pennsylvania. She had no idea what she was looking for; she was just looking. In the past, she had had a full-breed white shepherd and two mixed-breed shepherds. No matter what, she knew she was looking for puppies born on either the twenty-eighth or twenty-ninth of November.

Now that Hope was reborn, as I already had been told, I decided to contact her to obtain information to help us in our search for her. I needed some specifics. I readied myself in my meditation room, crystal in hand, as I called in all my spirit guides, animal totems, and Saint Francis to provide me with a clear communication to this wonderful puppy.

"Hope, I need to talk to you," I said as I pictured how she previously looked in my mind and held the essence of her determined heart in mine. I knew what it felt like when I was in contact with Hope, and I was praying it would be the same now that she was a puppy. I cleared my mind and sent her a picture of Rosanne with all the love I had in my heart for my friend. Sure enough, that did it!

"Hi, I'm here."

"Hi, Hope. I am so glad to talk with you again. Your family missed you so much. Can you tell me anything about where you are?"

"I am not sure where I am."

"What kind of dog are you?" I inquired.

"I'm a German shepherd. Mom likes them!"

I smiled at her statement. Her mom indeed loved German shepherds, as they were her favorite breed of dog.

"Me too. I love German shepherds." (I actually never met a dog I didn't adore, but she didn't need to know that. Besides, German shepherds did hold a special place in my heart from old childhood memory.) "Can you tell me anything about you that will help Mom find you?"

"I am mostly black. Mom didn't like the blonde fur on the couch, so I decided to come back the same color as Murray." Rosanne's other dog, Murray, was all black with curly hair. "Look into my eyes and soul, and you will see me," the puppy told me.

This was going to be harder than I thought.

"Okay, thank you so much, Hope. I will talk to you again real soon. But can you tell me, are you a boy or girl?"

"I don't know, how do I tell?"

Oh Lord, I did not expect this. I searched my brain for some way to answer her. *I know*, I thought. "Do you pee with a leg up?" That would surely indicate that the puppy was a boy.

"No. When I pee, I just hunker down a bit and let it go."

"Okay, thank you, Hope. We'll be in touch again real soon," I replied to her. Rats. Obviously puppies had no knowledge of their gender until later in life. I felt she was a girl, so I was going to count on my intuition and go with that. I didn't find out until later that all puppies squat to pee, and boys do not tend to lift their legs until later in life. Dumb me!

I called Rosanne with my information. She laughed, delighted that I was able to contact her and anxious as ever to bring her home. She really was tickled when I told her what Hope said about the fur, because she indeed had complained about the blonde fur as she was cleaning, and this conversation indicated that Hope remembered. I laughingly told her she was going to hell in a handbasket for that comment! Now more than ever, Rosanne was dying to find her dog.

"Relax. She is not ready to be separated from her mom and litter yet. We can't do anything for a while," I reminded Rosanne.

After the holiday season passed, Rosanne called to talk about finding Hope. Mitch had been searching online for dogs, but they didn't really know what they were looking for. Rosanne e-mailed me the information from the paper ads and searches the family had found on German shepherd puppies for sale. Rosanne had already called several of the ads to find out birth dates. Since we knew the actual date of her birth, it might be easier to pursue our quest using that information as it was the only substantial piece of data we had. Rosanne finally found three postings of pups born late November. Two of the postings were for German shepherd pups. The pictures provided showed all the pups were black and gray. The third posting was for a deliberate mix of a shepherd and something else. She was extremely puzzled that the search led to German shepherds. She read in an animal reincarnation book that most pets will usually reincarnate within the same breed and with your animal preferences. That being said, she pursued the article showing seven pups that were born on Wednesday, November 28, that were located in Pennsylvania. She e-mailed the owner of the puppies and received an e-mail back regarding her initial question. When she asked more specifics about the male dogs—all black, parents having large ears—and when could she see them, she never heard back from them. I told her that was a hint from the universe not to bother with them.

Rosanne was hot on the trail, and she would not be deterred. The second advertisement was for a litter of eleven pups in Akron, Ohio. She e-mailed them, "Hello, I am inquiring about the adorable pups you have for sale. Do you have a picture of their mom and dad? Do you have a mostly black male not accounted for? Do you schedule a viewing time to meet the pups and select one? Were the pups born in the early morning of the twenty-ninth?" She received her answers. This litter sounded promising, but she needed more guidance.

"How do I know where to find her, Diane?" Rosanne inquired during one of our many phone calls. "Is she in the United States?"

"Um, let's see if I can get information regarding that question." I closed my eyes, called in my guides, Saint Francis, and my totem animals and asked them if the new puppy that was Hope reincarnated could be found in the United States. I received an affirmative answer, which made me very happy. I told Rosanne, "Yes. The dog we seek is in the United States."

"Okay, what state is Hope in? Will I have to travel far to find her, like Pennsylvania?"

I concentrated on that question and heard, "No, she is here in Ohio." *Oh, good*, I thought. *That is a relief.* I proceeded to tell

Rosanne that she could be found in Ohio. Rosanne seemed very happy that we would not have to travel too far, because none of us knew how this was all going to unfold.

Rosanne, so persistent, asked, "If she is in Ohio, where in Ohio is she? What city?"

Again I did my thing and saw a big letter *C*. Okay, I could work with that. I told Rosanne, "I see the letter *C*, so it could be Canton, Cleveland, Chagrin Falls, Columbus or any number of cities. We have lots of choices! Are any of the ads that you have located in a city that begins with the letter *C*?"

Her response was a depressing, "No cities beginning with the letter *C*."

Rats, I thought. This was not promising. Rosanne had more phone calls to make, so we wrapped up our call about the miracle unfolding before us.

When I closed my eyes in attempt to sleep that night, I heard someone say to me, "You know, Diane, the *C* could be a street name or the beginning of the last name of who has the dog you seek." My eyes shot wide open. *Oh, crap!* I was being too closed-minded about this whole endeavor. Now we had more choices, but I knew my guides told me this information for a reason. In this statement was a clue to the answer I was looking for, if only I could find it. I could not wait until the morning. I had to call Rosanne and tell her my news. Boy, I'd never be able to do this on my own. I certainly needed my spirit guides. I closed my eyes and thanked them profusely for this nugget of information. *They are too sly*, I thought. They usually don't provide the exact information you require; they lead you to your answer. It's all very cryptic and like a puzzle of sorts. I always will wonder why they do it that way. I guess it's all about the free will thing.

The next morning, bright and early, I was on the phone with Rosanne telling her about my revelation from last night. I said,

"Contact the people you had from Akron, the one that stated the puppies were born on the day we know Hope was born. Find out the name of the street they live on or their last name, and then call me immediately." After we disconnected, I sat, hoping that these people she was calling would answer her questions and not think she was stalking them or something worse. After all, we were getting very personal in our line of questioning, but we had to know.

Rosanne finally heard back from the people in Akron. They said that their litter was born on Thursday, November 29, in the early morning. All the girls were born first and then the boys. The mother dog's contractions began on Wednesday, November 28, but the babies waited until Thursday before entering the world. In addition to this information, she found out the most amazing fact of all when they answered her e-mail. Their last name began with a *C*.

When Rosanne called me back my mouth fell open in wonder at her news. "I could tell she was about to explode with excitement. "The people in Akron—their last name is *Cutbin.*"

Oh Lord, I thought, *it's all coming together.* I could hardly believe my ears. "Fabulous," I replied. "Make an appointment, and I will go with you."

Rosanne received an appointment to see the pups on Sunday, January 6, the next day, in the early afternoon. Off we went, Rosanne, Mitch, and me, on the adventure of a lifetime. It seemed to take forever to arrive; however, it truly was only about thirty minutes away from my house. We chatted nervously about our expectations and what we might find. I had in my brain that I would stand back and not participate much in this part of the process. I wanted Rosanne to find her dog for herself. Hope had said that she would be recognized by looking into her soul and eyes, along with her stand-up ears, and I felt Rosanne and Mitch were the people to do that, not me! With that settled in my mind, I sat back and prayed for this family to find their beloved pet again.

Rosanne's heart was beating so fast that she thought she could hear her blood flowing through her ears. Once we arrived, we were greeted by an adorable elderly couple, who escorted us to a large heated garage on their property. The mother of the puppies came out to greet us along with one of her pups from a previous litter. The dogs were huge! I was astounded as to how big these German shepherds were. I could not wait to see the puppies. The minute they opened the door, a large group of beautiful, tiny, black-and-gray puppies all yipped for attention. The Cutbin family had fashioned a makeshift playpen, like a sandbox minus the sand, in their heated garage for the dogs. The puppies were all happily playing. The walls of the pen were plywood and were at least two feet high. I was enthralled. There were eleven puppies in total, all wiggling bundles of energy and joy. The grin hit my face and never left.

I immediately stooped down and picked up a beautiful puppy in my arms to cuddle. I buried my nose in its fur. Nothing like the smell of puppies! They have a distinct odor that, if I could, I would wear as perfume. Okay, I know I am nuts, but let's face it, I probably smell like an animal, anyway, between my horse, dog, and cat.

They were confined in this large wooden pen and were climbing all over each other to get to us. It was overwhelming. Rosanne stood staring at all the puppies, not sure what to do.

Rosanne and Mitch smiled and chatted with the owners as they surveyed all the pups. Rosanne began picking up pups that were looking up at her from the pen. There were some pups that couldn't care less that we were there. Both Rosanne and Mitch seemed to be looking for something in particular, but I really didn't pay them too much attention. I was in heaven! I had never had the opportunity to cuddle with so many puppies. Any pup who came up to me was lavished with hugs and kisses. They were all adorable! After the third pup Rosanne scooped up in her arms, she began to feel confused. It is hard to listen to your instincts when your emotions are flying off the rocker. It was a little girl, who gave her a single kiss on the lips, but again, she was unsure because she did not keep Rosanne's gaze and the puppy started squirming in her arms to be put down. She couldn't tell if it was Hope. She didn't seem to have the "wow" moment she was looking for. Meanwhile, I was so wrapped up in my own ecstasy that I didn't realize that Rosanne seemed in distress until I looked over at her with a big silly grin on my face. My smile faded. She looked panicked, and Mitch didn't look much better. She seemed overwhelmed. Rosanne had been picking up different puppies, looking deeply into their eyes, and so had Mitch, but they didn't seem to find what they were searching for. She whispered to me, "I don't know. What should I do?"

I decided right there and then that the animal communicator needed to step in for a minute. I put down the puppy that I was holding, closed my eyes, and said my usual prayers for guidance and clarity. I probably sounded a little panicked at this point, too, as I didn't want to let Rosanne and her family down. I silently called, "Hope, are you here?"

I waited a minute, and a small little voice said, "Yes, I am here."

I opened my eyes to survey the milling puppies. *Where?* I thought. I did the only thing I could think of. I placed my hands down into the pen with my arms wide open and quietly said, "Hope, come to me now."

I was astonished when a little puppy, mostly black, came forward from the back of the pen where she was playing with another puppy, walked right up to where my hands were and jumped up against the pen walls. Her front paws perched on the wood between my hands as she seemed to be begging for me to pick her up. My mouth fell open as I immediately scooped up this little bundle of joy. I looked directly into her face and said, "Are you Hope?"

"Yes, I am," came an immediate answer. I hugged her for a very brief moment and then looked over at Rosanne, my heart full. She had another dog in her arms and was looking very disappointed and sad, almost in pain. I removed that dog from her hands, shaking my head slightly and placed Hope in her arms. She stared at the pup that I handed her. It was a little girl who was extremely quiet, not wiggling around, who stared back at her while in her arms and then gently gave Rosanne a single kiss on her nose. Rosanne's eyes filled up so fast that she couldn't see the puppy, and she hugged her tightly.

Little did I know that Hope and Rosanne had made a pact before she passed away that Hope would give a specific sign to Rosanne so that she could recognize her. Rosanne never shared this information with me. She had asked Hope, in prayer, if Hope would identify herself when Rosanne was holding her by looking lovingly into her eyes and giving her one tiny, soft kiss on the nose. Hope looked deeply into Rosanne's eyes, and I heard her say, "Here I am, Mom." After the little dog gently kissed Rosanne directly on the nose, the smile that split Rosanne's face could have lit up New York. She was crying and laughing at the same time as the tears poured down her cheek. She started bestowing the many kisses that she had been saving since Hope had left her onto the little puppy's head.

The love and emotion that I felt caused tears to fill my eyes too. Just seeing them together again made my heart sing in a way that it will probably never do again. I can't even describe the feeling, as it was pure magic. At that moment, the puppy looked at Mitch over Rosanne's shoulder and then let out a squeal and wiggled to get to him. Rosanne passed her over to Mitch. At this point, the puppy was so excited that she was dancing in his arms and smothering him with kisses. He broke into a huge smile, knowing in his heart that this was his dog. They had found each other again.

The family witnessed two signs at that moment, proving that this little pup was indeed Hope, but it was the third sign that gave the stamp of approval. The litter's owner, out of the blue, mentioned to us that the pup Mitch was now holding was the first one in the litter whose ears stood up. This was Hope's signature, her ears. She had said we would recognize her by her ears. Rosanne and I looked at each other with stupid, happy grins on our faces. *Naturally,* I thought, *that is exactly how Hope told us we would recognize her when she returned, by her stand-up ears that were uniquely Hope!* We definitely had the right dog!

We all started talking at once. Rosanne began by saying this was the puppy she was choosing and inquired what they had to do to seal the deal with Mrs. Cutbin.

The litter's owners told us that the puppies were still two weeks too young, and we would have to come back to pick her up. Rosanne looked like someone stabbed her in the heart but reluctantly agreed. What could we do? Rules are rules! Mrs. Cutbin picked a hand-knitted little pink collar for the chosen puppy and placed it on her neck. She said, "This will let us know which puppy is yours when you come back to claim her."

We stayed and played some more with the puppies as Rosanne transacted the biggest deal of her life with the owners. Checks and congratulations were exchanged along with phone numbers and the date to return to pick up Hope. I hated to leave, as I was having the time of my life, hugging all the pups and being licked head to toe. Rosanne and Mitch reluctantly returned Hope, now to be named Faith, to her littermates and watched as she played with the others. *So this is what reincarnation feels like,* I thought. I'd have to participate in this type of animal communication more often, as I felt so peaceful and happy. I knew a miracle had indeed just occurred, and I knew I was an active player in the event. I imagined that nothing could ever feel that satisfying again. The emotion was overwhelmingly wonderful. I would definitely make it my mission to try to bring pets and their families back together. I learned a very valuable life lesson that day that will never leave me. Thank you, Rosanne and Faith!

The ride home was like a jubilant party without the liquor, everyone talking excitedly about what had occurred and how they felt. We were all ecstatic over finding our *Faith,* literally! I was dropped off at my house late in the afternoon with a sense of accomplishment and love in my heart. We had come full circle, and it was amazing. I couldn't wait to tell my husband and family all about it. I could barely sleep that night, and I was sure that Rosanne never closed her eyes. I was as excited as she was. To see this scenario unfold before my eyes was mind-blowing. I could not express my gratitude to the universe on how awesome it was to work so perfectly with us. We were indeed very blessed.

Unfortunately, nothing worth having is ever that easy, and the next day proved this saying to be true. Rosanne received a called from Mrs. Cutbin stating that the puppies had pulled the collar off of her selected pup during the night, and she didn't know which one Rosanne wanted.

Rosanne immediately called me in a panic. As she explained to me what happened, I thought she was close to an emotional breakdown. I was flabbergasted at the turn of events but wanted to remain confident for Rosanne's sake. We both started to worry all over again. I wondered if this was a sign from the universe or something that I missed. I called in my guides and animal totems along with Saint Francis to help guide us to find Hope yet again. This pup sure was elusive!

I told her to book an appointment to go back to find our puppy as soon as possible, and I would drop everything to be at her disposal. Rosanne forgot to mention to Mrs. Cutbin the important fact that the puppy she selected was the puppy whose ears went up first. The Cutbins were willing to let the dog go early, but I had to be at the animal shelter the later part of Monday and couldn't go. We scheduled to go back on Tuesday. We had to wait until the Cutbins returned from the vet. All eleven pups were getting the dewormed.

Down we traveled to Akron to the Cutbin house, Rosanne, Mitch, and me, not talking too much, as we were all caught up in our own thoughts. I knew this was meant to be, and we had the right dog; we just had to find her again. No problem, right? I hoped I was oozing confidence that I didn't have.

We were forewarned to arrive before the male dog breeder arrived, because he was picking out his pups that very day. When we arrived, the breeder had beat us to the house, but Rosanne blocked his truck in the driveway, and we all raced into the garage to see if he had tried to take Hope.

Here we go again, I thought to myself. I waited to take my cue from Rosanne, hoping that she would be able to find her dog again. She picked up one puppy, looked into its eyes, and shook her head. Placing the pup back into the litter, she obtained another dog. Again, she held the dog in her arms with such anticipation on her face, only to be sadly disappointed. I could practically feel her desperation. A little girl pup ran in front of her, which in her fear of losing her again, she thought was Hope. Once her nerves calmed down, she began to question herself.

I am sure the breeder did not know what to make of us crazy ladies, picking up one puppy after another only to put them back with their littermates. Finally, I had had enough. I decided to take control of the situation and do what I do best. I had Rosanne return all the puppies to the pen, shook my head at her when she looked questioningly at me, and silently called out for Hope. "Hope, please come to me!" I implored as I stretched out my arms and hands again into the pen full of wiggling, playing puppies. A puppy started to make her way toward me, and I watched carefully to see where she was going. Sure enough, as Rosanne stood next to me, watching with wide eyes, the puppy came right up to me. She placed her paws on the top of the pen, right between my outstretched hands and looked up at me, longingly, begging to be picked up. The look in her eyes went right through to my soul. I picked her up lovingly and cuddled her for a second as I silently said, "Hope, is this you?"

The little voice came to me was like music to my ears. "Yes, you have me." I blinked back my tears and, with a huge smile on my face, presented Hope to Rosanne. As I placed her beloved dog reverently into her arms, the tears were already rolling down Rosanne's face, but I couldn't cry. I was overjoyed. Hope was true to her promise to her mom and immediately softly kissed her nose in greeting, as to say, "Here I am again!" From the look on her face, I knew Rosanne had found her heart's desire, so I quietly leaned into both of them and whispered, "Don't let that dog out of your arms!" Rosanne bobbed her head in agreement. I began to doubt if we would be able to pry the dog from her!

There was no question that we had Hope when Mitch disappeared from the garage to play with one of the larger pups from a previous litter and Hope began to yip. We had to call Mitch back into the garage, because it was the only way Hope would calm down. Rosanne placed her on the ground next to Mitch, and she immediately began to follow him around.

Mr. and Mrs. Cutbin felt so bad about the mix-up that they graciously agreed to let Rosanne take her puppy home immediately with her. Rosanne handed the puppy over to Mitch for safekeeping as she concluded her business transaction with the Cutbin family. I took advantage of everyone being busy and began to play with all the other puppies. I don't have the opportunity too often to indulge myself in puppy play; therefore, I was going to take advantage of the situation yet again. They could take all day for all I cared.

We talked some more to the family, promising pictures to be sent as we readied to leave. As we were getting into the car, with Rosanne driving, she bestowed upon me the greatest honor. I was to hold the wiggling Hope/Faith in my arms all the way home. With a grin as wide as the Grand Canyon, I prayed for a lot of traffic to lengthen our trip. She was just so sweet and adorable. Faith fell asleep in my arms. *Oh, what an angel*, I thought as she dozed away. I kept putting my nose down to her head to breathe in that unique puppy smell that I love so much.

Once we arrived back at my house, we decided to let Faith down to have some water and to have a potty break. Rosanne still had at least a twenty- to twenty-five-minute drive back to her house, and we wanted Faith to be as comfortable as possible. As Faith bounced around the yard, my husband came to the door, grinning.

"Ah, so this is what all the fuss has been about," he said. "Kind of small for all the trouble she caused!"

We all smiled at him, too delighted to finally have her back in our lives to pay his teasing any attention.

Once Rosanne finally got home with Faith, the other family pets—Murray, Apollo, and Callie—greeted her at the door with tons of kisses. Rosanne took Faith into the sitting room to see the Christmas tree. Yes, she had kept the recent Christmas tree up for Faith, because Hope loved Christmas, and the family did not want her to miss a year of presents and the pleasure of a tree. Faith smelled the tree and then bounced between Rosanne's and Mitch's laps as they helped her open her presents. It was like she had always been there and nothing had happened. But it did. They had a miracle, just like Rosanne asked for in her prayers when Hope was sick. She had asked for a miracle for Hope, and she received one.

The other family pets all seemed to recognize Hope in the new dog. Faith greeted each one of them as if to say, "See, I am back." She made herself right at home, as if she'd never left. She knew where the food bowls were, where she had to go out to relieve herself, and where she was allowed to sleep. Amazing dog!

Faith has many traits of Hope; however, she is her own special being with many new traits. She is a loving dog, but protective, and has playdates with many dogs. This is a practice that the family wished they could have provided to Hope, but she would not cooperate. Faith has been professionally trained, but there are days you cannot tell. After all, she is still very much a puppy. She uses her paws like hands, just like Hope. She swiped what was left of her favorite toy along with her bone from Rosanne's bedroom, somehow remembering this belonged to her when she was called Hope. Only a leg from her blue stuffed toy remained, but she still loves it, along with the original bone she always had. Most of all, she gives beautiful, soft kisses and lets everyone know who her mommy is, which is just perfect with Rosanne.

Afterword

N ot all pets reincarnate. Please do not expect that. However, just like our human family members, we miraculously seem to maintain our soul-to-soul connections within our family group, no matter if they are human or animal. This is wonderful news for anyone looking for a beloved pet to return to them. I have personally witnessed it time and time again as I speak with your animal family members. Many animals tell me that they have been with their owners in past lives and even go on to explain how they worked in harmony with each other. The idea that we never really lose our loved ones, human or animal, is truly a blessing.

I believe we owe it to our beloved animal friends to provide comfort and healing where we can. After all, as pet owners, we are responsible for their health and well-being. When you actually participate to provide healing, you will promote a closer relationship between you and your pet companion. Throughout your pet's life and through years of love and dedication to our animal friends, you can help your animal companion become happier and healthier and improve their quality of life by getting involved with the healing process yourself.

Remember, our bodies have wonderful abilities to restore themselves into balance. We can facilitate that process by using holistic methods, along with traditional medicine to ensure that both we and those we love are operating at our best. I hope you and your pets find each other along with a pot of good health at the end of the rainbow. Don't forget to have love, hope, and above all, faith!

Reunited

Diane Weinmann

When first we met,
Your eyes held mine,
Our hearts entwined
Forever.
You placed your trust in me
And didn't let me down.
We made memories together,
Soul to Soul,
Forever,
Never to part.
If only love could make it so,
Forever.
Our days were fleeting,
No matter how long it seemed,
Until our eyes held for the last time,
Heart to heart,
Soul to Soul
A promise given—
Undying love—
To return someday to share again
Forever,
Reunited.

If you would like a bookmark with this poem on it, please e-mail
me at DianeTailofHopesFaith@aol.com and provide your address.
I will mail it to you.

With love,
Diane

Additional Resources

Bach Flower Essences and how they can help

Aspen—helps manage the fear of unknown things

Beech—helps to make pet have more tolerance with other pets and people

Cherry Plum—helps the animal be self-controlled

Chestnut Bud—helps with the pet if he/she fails to learn from mistakes

Chicory—helps correct selfishness, possessive love of objects, other animal or people

Clematis—helps pet who has become uninterested in life to be more present in the day and to enjoy the world

Crab Apple—the cleansing remedy to be used when pet is overgrooming

Elm—helps restore confidence and positive outlook to a pet overwhelmed by responsibility

Gentian—helps to manage discouragement after a setback; can be used for pets who have been ill for long periods of time

Gorse—helps to correct hopelessness and despair

Heather—helps a pet that is clingy, barking a lot; helps animal to not need to be the center of attention

Holly—helps to manage hatred, envy, and jealousy; helps pet share with others and to be fine when there are many animals in household

Honeysuckle—helps to correct homesickness, loss of owner or home; helps pet adjust to changes and environment

Hornbeam—restores vitality in lethargic animals

Impatiens—restores patience in animals

Larch—helps to correct the lack of confidence in performance, restores self-confidence; perfect for show animals

Mimulus—helps conquer fear of known things

Mustard—manages deep gloom for no reason; pet seems depressed

Oak—corrects the animal that keeps going past the point of exhaustion

Olive—manages exhaustion following mental or physical effort; good for animals doing any type of physical work or shows

Pine—helps to manage guilt

Red Chestnut—helps to correct overconcern for the welfare of loved ones

Vervain—help when pets are high strung, helps pets to relax

Vine—helps pets that are dominant to be not so domineering

Walnut—helps facilitate any change

Water Violet—helps pets that are unfriendly or standoffish to become more affectionate and sociable

Healing with Colors

Color can help you heal yourself or others. You can breathe in the color you wish to project and then push the color out through your hands or breathe onto the animal or person. You can use color lights, cloth, or cellophane to assist you in bring color into someone's energy field. Set your intention, and know that you will succeed. Different colors will help with specific health issues. The key is how to know what color to use. The list below will help you determine the appropriate color to choose for your healing experience. Remember, if you do not know what the emotional or physical problem is, just send white or the rainbow.

Red—energizes, warms, helps with sinuses and colds or to dry your mucous membrane, acne, anemia, low blood pressure, hay fever

Orange—balances your emotions, helps with creativity, replenishes joy, helps respiratory conditions; pale orange for muscle ache, asthma, bladder issues, hay fever

Yellow—helps with gas and indigestion, cramps, enables you to learn easily, inner head issues, loss of appetite, alcoholism, bladder issues, burping

Green—helps with nervous conditions, helps lessen bad habits, provide a sense of prosperity, improvement to your vision, headache, bleeding, heart issues, nerves, ulcers

Pink—helps with skin problems and puffiness, combats loneliness, heart issues

Blue—calms, helps with artistic endeavors, generally good for healing children, eases respiratory conditions, abscesses, headache and toothache; light blue for anxieties, asthma, bleeding, high blood pressure, burns, bronchitis, fever

Indigo—helps heal after surgery, revives intuition, treats alcoholism, eyes

Teal—heals bones

Turquoise—respiratory problems, arthritis, earache, epilepsy, flu

Violet—skeletal issues, purifying, detox, helps bring about spiritual awakening; use for arthritis, bones, diabetes, growths, infection, flu, leukemia

Purple—helps to fight strong obsessions and negative feelings, detoxifying

Specific issues

Pneumonia—red with red-orange combined with indigo

Cancer—Blue, blue violet, followed by pink

Liver—blue and yellow combinations

AIDS—red, indigo, violet, followed by pink and gold

Alzheimer's disease—royal blue, blue purple, followed by yellow

Links

Lumalights—healing with color lights
http://www.spectrahue.com/

Healing Touch for Animals
http://www.healingtouchforanimals.com/

You can purchase tuning forks from this website:
Inner Sound—Tuning Forks
http://innersoundonline.com

To purchase light pads:
http://www.CanineLightTherapy.com
http://www.EquineLightTherapy.com

Animal Hospice in Cleveland, Ohio, area
http://www.joycares.com

Dan Sumerel—STS-2 System
http://sumereltraining.com/therapy.htm

Animals in Our Hearts—Teresa Wagner (Pet Loss Grief Support and Animal Communication)
http://www.animalsinourhearts.com/

Diane Weinmann—For the Love of Animals (Animal Communication and Holistic Healing)
http://www.theloveofanimals.com/

About the Author

I found out I could talk to animals when I began to regularly talk to my first horse, Cheemo. I used to tell everyone, especially the kids who came to visit, that he could talk just like Mr. Ed, the famous "talking" horse. I knew I heard what Cheemo was telling me in my head, and I actually thought that was normal. It took me a long time to realize that not everyone could do this.

I always had a rapport with animals that was, let's say, unusual, like we were of one mind. I assumed everyone was like that too. I've been psychic all my life, a gift passed down from my grandmother and mom. Bless them! It is by far the best gift I have ever had, other than my son and husband.

As a teenager, I noticed that I began to "see" movies or visions right in front of me, but whatever I saw was not really happening right then. It actually happened later in the day. Freaky! I got used to that too. When I "saw" someone get hit by a car, and five minutes later, they actually did, I decided that I would *never* second-guess or ignore what I was witnessing. Yes, the person died (not right then but later that day), and I will live with that guilt for the rest of my life.

Another trauma I will carry with me forever was when my horse called to me in the early evening, and I, again, just thought she was thinking of me. I had been to visit her earlier in the day, and everything was fine. My family and I were just on our way to pick up a video to watch, and I *knew* my husband would never go for visiting the barn a second time on the same day, so I kept quiet. Approximately three hours later, we got a phone call that my husband took. He had a strange look on his face when he rejoined us for the rest of the movie, so I made him promise that nothing was wrong with my family. At the time, my mom was ill with cancer. He assured me that nothing was wrong with my family. About thirty minutes later, our doorbell rang, and my twin sister was at the door. Both of them together told me that the barn had burned down, and all sixteen horses had died; that was what the phone call was all about. Needless to say, I had to be sedated.

I tell you about these tragedies since I will never be the same because of them. I learned a great deal about my gift, honoring it and never doubting. I only wish the knowledge had come to me in such a way that others would not have had to suffer, but I do not control the universe or God. Through the years of my talking to animals, I have realized that our beloved companions are a constant source of joy. They help us heal physically by lowering blood pressure and reducing stress and related physical problems while they provide unconditional love and loyalty.

With the use of interspecies telepathic communication, I help companion animals to have a voice. I've learned how animals think and perceive the world. Together, we come to an "agreement" on many different types of issues, healing on different levels and promoting a closer relationship between you and your pet companion. As we communicate, I sense if they are in need of healing in physical, emotional, or spiritual terms. Their cries for help led me to study Reiki, Healing Touch for Animals (HTA), TTouch, tuning forks, Bach Flower Essences, Essential oils aromatherapy, healing with color (Color Harmonics), and the STS-2 light system.

My animal communication / physic gift was developed with the help of my teacher and mentor, Theresa. Over many years of training, a lot of laughter, and many tears, Theresa taught me to control my gift, how to call upon it when I need it, and how to silence it when necessary. I am forever in her debt, as the service she provided was unprecedented compared to any other training I received. Theresa, along with my healing group, helped make me the person I am today, and that debt can never be repaid. I thank them all from the bottom of my heart.

As you can see, the services I provide come from years of love, training, and dedication to our animal friends. Together, I feel we can help your animal companions become happier and healthier and improve their quality of life.

Animal Communications

I have worked in the telepathic animal communication field for over eleven years. I voice concerns for both living and deceased animals that want to be heard. I have studied animal communications under the direction of Dr. Agnes Thomas, who obtained her PhD from Case Western Reserve University. She is recognized nationally for her work in brain development research and development of respiratory control. She is also the author of *Pets Tell the Truth* and *Animals Tell the Truth Wisdom Cards.*

I've learned to listen to the animals' communications about their physical and mental health. I've also learned animal anatomy and how to have the animal show me the inside of its body and identify problem areas. In addition, I am well versed in handling behavior problems, death, the dying process, and lost animals.

Reiki

I practice Reiki at the master level and began my Reiki journey in 2005. Reiki is a Japanese method of healing; the term represents universal life energy, which is all around us. Applied for the purpose of healing, Reiki accelerates the body's ability to heal physical ailments and opens the mind and spirit. The Usui system of Reiki is a natural healing art that uses Reiki in those ways. Reiki is administered by "laying of hands" and is based on the idea that an unseen life force energy flows through us and causes us to be alive. If the life force energy is low, we are more prone to sickness and so on. If the energy is high, we are more capable of being stress-free, healthy, and happy.

Healing Touch for Animals (HTA)

I have practiced Healing Touch for Animals (HTA) since 2005. I use the bioenergy field of the animal's body to promote wellness. HTA is at the forefront of holistic animal health care. It provides specific energy techniques and a hands-on application that works on all species of animals. HTA uses basic science to maintain and regulate a healthy immune system for animals. Under the Komitor healing method, I have completed all four levels of HTA.

Color Harmonics

I have worked with color to heal people and pets since 2008. Color harmonics is used to promote wellness in you and your pet. The Lumalight uses color therapy as an energy healing-based modality. Color therapy has been known to strengthen, cleanse, invigorate, and balance and may regulate metabolic processes, positively influencing bodily functions and moods. Our animal's meridian system has energy channels for the body, activated by light. The Lumalight system was developed by Julianne Bien, founder of Spectrahue Light & Sound, Inc. Through direct study with Julianne Bien, I have discovered the science, theory, and practical application of color light. Julianne has been harnessing the nutritional aspects of color as it provides emotional, physical, antiaging, and spiritual benefits. She is the author of *Golden Light: A Journey with Advanced Colorworks* and *Color: Awakening the Child Within*.

TTouch

Tellington TTouch is a gentle hands-on method that develops a deep understanding of animals and humans. I began my course of study with this healing technique in 2009 and have used it quite often in my animal communication/healing business. It is helpful for any being with a nervous system. It can improve behavior, enhance healing and health, develop the ability to learn without fear or force, and deepen the bond between you and your animal. The TTouch is essentially bodywork that includes circular movements and lifts all over the animal's body. The intent of TTouch is to work at the cellular level to increase an animal's awareness and enable them to learn and focus.

STS-2 Healing with Color System

I purchased the STS-2 healing system many years ago and basically taught myself how to heal with this system, using educational videos and books supplied by the inventor and many telephone calls between me and him. The STS-2 healing system is a two-part process. The scanner allows me to physically scan an animal's body externally and specifically locate where any problems exist, because the scanner has the ability to locate acupuncture points and flag where there are issues. The light portion of the healing system has twenty-four infrared and twenty-five red LEDs. The system allows me to program both the frequency and time exposure for the optimal healing effect. The light therapy will stimulate immediately, but often the improvements will continue for forty-eight to seventy-two hours. You can buy something similar to the light pad I used from a company called Canine Light Therapy and Equine Light Therapy or purchase the exact one I used from Dan Sumerel. Please see the additional resource section for their websites.

Bach Flower Essences

I have been working with Bach Flower Essences since 2003 in my animal communication and healing business for treating emotional and behavioral problems with my clients. My standard behavioral evaluation asks clients to answer questions on the emotional health of their pets. This is followed by a discussion with the pet as I evaluate him or her. At the conclusion of the consultation, I provide the client with a plan to talk with his or her pet in combination with essences for the pet's specific emotional profile. I usually use both behavior modification and Bach Flower Essences, because it has been my experience that the use of the essences can shorten the amount of time for a given behavior modification protocol. I have also treated some cases only with essences and have seen dramatic results.

Essential Oils Aromatherapy

I began my journey with essential oils in 2006 in my Healing Touch for Animal classes, and I have witnessed many dramatic changes in an animal's behavior, thanks to their use. I furthered my education with a certification in aromatherapy in 2012. Aromatherapy is a form of alternative medicine that uses volatile plant materials, known as essential oils, and other aromatic compounds for the purpose of altering a person's or pet's mind, mood, cognitive function, or health. Aromatherapy is the treatment or prevention of disease by use of essential oils. Other uses include pain and anxiety reduction, enhancement of energy and short-term memory, relaxation, hair-loss prevention, and reduction of eczema-induced itching. Essential oils can assist animals with their healing using energetic vibration and the essence of the natural product. They can help bring balance and healing through their sense of smell, which is the most receptive of the pet's systems. The oil stimulates the olfactory system, which in turn sends a signal to the brain regarding the specific oil. The brain then activates the pet's natural ability to begin the healing process. Aromatherapy does not cure conditions but helps the body to find a natural way to cure itself and improve immune response.

Tuning Forks

I developed my love of tuning forks when I learned Healing Touch for Animals (HTA) in 2003. They are my go-to technique to create relaxation and a quick fix for issues pets may have with trust and with their physical bodies. Tuning forks are used for both sound and vibrational therapy. Vibrational therapy is accomplished by placing the forks on the body (bones, spine, joint) to create balance in the energy system. Sound therapy helps integrate other healing that is offered at a deeper level, and the sound helps to settle and ground the animal.